Python Prograr

Paperback printed edition setup on Createspace by D. Bill Platypus

ISBN-13: 978-1466366053

Contents

Articles

Modules

References

Article Licenses

Learning Python

Python Programming/Overview

Index		Next: Getting Python

Python is a high-level, structured, open-source programming language that can be used for a wide variety of programming tasks. It is good for simple quick-and-dirty scripts, as well as complex and intricate applications.

It is an interpreted programming language that is automatically compiled into bytecode before execution (the bytecode is then normally saved to disk, just as automatically, so that compilation need not happen again until and unless the source gets changed). It is also a dynamically typed language that includes (but does not require one to use) object oriented features and constructs.

The most unusual aspect of Python is that whitespace is significant; instead of block delimiters (braces → "{ }" in the C family of languages), indentation is used to indicate where blocks begin and end.

For example, the following Python code can be interactively typed at an interpreter prompt, to display the beginning values in the Fibonacci series:

```
>>> a,b = 0,1
>>> print(b)
1
>>> while b < 100:
...     a,b = b,(a+b)
...     print(b, end=" ")
...
1 2 3 5 8 13 21 34 55 89 144
```

Another interesting aspect in Python is reflection and introspection. The **dir()** function returns the list of the names of objects in the current scope. However, **dir(object)** will return the names of the attributes of the specified object. The **locals()** routine returns a dictionary in which the names in the local namespace are the keys and their values are the objects to which the names refer. Combined with the interactive interpreter, this provides a useful environment for exploration and prototyping.

Python provides a powerful assortment of built-in types (e.g., lists, dictionaries and strings), a number of built-in functions, and a few constructs, mostly statements. For example, loop constructs that can iterate over items in a collection instead of being limited to a simple range of integer values. Python also comes with a powerful standard library, which includes hundreds of modules to provide routines for a wide variety of services including regular expressions and TCP/IP sessions.

Python is used and supported by a large Python Community [1] that exists on the Internet. The mailing lists and news groups [2] like the tutor list [3] actively support and help new python programmers. While they discourage doing homework for you, they are quite helpful and are populated by the authors of many of the Python textbooks currently available on the market. It is named after Monty Python's Flying Circus comedy program, and created by Guido Van Rossum.

Index		Next: Getting Python

References

[1] http://www.python.org/community/index.html

[2] http://www.python.org/community/lists.html

[3] http://mail.python.org/mailman/listinfo/tutor

Python Programming/Getting Python

Previous: Overview	Index	Next: Setting it up

In order to program in Python you need the Python interpreter. If it is not already installed or if the version you are using is obsolete, you will need to obtain and install Python using the methods below:

Installing Python in Windows

Go to the Python Homepage [1] or the ActiveState website [2] and get the proper version for your platform. Download it, read the instructions and get it installed.

In order to run Python from the command line, you will need to have the python directory in your PATH. Alternatively, you could use an Integrated Development Environment (IDE) for Python like DrPython[3], eric[4], PyScripter[5], or Python's own IDLE (which ships with every version of Python since 2.3).

The PATH variable can be modified from the Window's System control panel. The advanced tab will contain the button labelled *Environment Variables*, where you can append the newly created folder to the search path.

If you prefer having a temporary environment, you can create a new command prompt short-cut that automatically executes the following statement:

```
PATH %PATH%;c:\python26
```

If you downloaded a different version (such as Python 3.1), change the "26" for the version of Python you have (26 is 2.6.x, the current version of Python 2.)

Cygwin

By default, the Cygwin installer for Windows does not include Python in the downloads. However, it can be selected from the list of packages.

Installing Python on Mac

Users on Apple Mac OS X will find that it already ships with Python 2.3 (OS X 10.4 Tiger), but if you want the more recent version head to Python Download Page [6] follow the instruction on the page and in the installers. As a bonus you will also install the Python IDE.

Installing Python on Unix environments

Python is available as a package for some Linux distributions. In some cases, the distribution CD will contain the python package for installation, while other distributions require downloading the source code and using the compilation scripts.

Gentoo GNU/Linux

Gentoo is an example of a distribution that installs Python by default - the package system *Portage* depends on Python.

Ubuntu GNU/Linux

Users of Ubuntu 6.06 (Dapper Drake) and earlier will notice that Python comes installed by default, only it sometimes is not the latest version. If you would like to update it, just open a terminal and type at the prompt:

```
$ sudo apt-get update   # This will update the software repository
$ sudo apt-get install python   # This one will actually install python
```

Arch GNU/Linux

Arch does not install python by default, but is easily available for installation through the package manager to pacman. As root (or using sudo if you've installed and configured it), type:

```
$ pacman -Sy python
```

This will be update package databases and install python. Other versions can be built from source from the Arch User Repository.

Source code installations

Some platforms do not have a version of Python installed, and do not have pre-compiled binaries. In these cases, you will need to download the source code from the official site [1]. Once the download is complete, you will need to unpack the compressed archive into a folder.

To build Python, simply run the configure script (requires the Bash shell) and compile using make.

Previous: Overview	Index	Next: Setting it up

References

[1] http://www.python.org/download/
[2] http://activestate.com
[3] http://drpython.sourceforge.net/
[4] http://www.die-offenbachs.de/eric/index.html
[5] http://mmm-experts.com/Products.aspx?ProductID=4
[6] http://www.python.org/download/mac

Python Programming/Setting it up

Previous: Getting Python	Index	Next: Interactive mode

Installing Python PyDEV Plug-in for Eclipse IDE

You can use the Eclipse IDE as your Python IDE. The only requirement is Eclipse and the Eclipse PyDEV Plug-in.

Go to http://www.eclipse.org/downloads/and get the proper Eclipse IDE version for your OS platform. There are also updates on the site but, just look for the basic program, Download and install it. The install just requires you to unpack the downloaded Eclipse install file onto your system.

You can install PyDEV Plug-in two ways:

- **Suggested:** Use Eclipse's update manager, found in the tool bar under "Help" -> "install new Software". add http://pydev.org/updates/in "work with" clik add, and select PyDEV and let Eclipse do the rest. Eclipse will now check for any updates to PyDEV when it searches for updates.
  - If you get an error stating a requirement for the plugin "org.eclipse.mylyn", expand the PyDEV tree, and deselect the optional mylyn components.
- Or install PyDEV manually, by going to http://pydev.sourceforge.net and get the latest PyDEV Plug-in version. Download it, and install it by unpacking it into the Eclipse base folder.

Python Mode for Emacs

There is also a python mode for Emacs which provides features such as running pieces of code, and changing the tab level for blocks. You can download the mode at https://launchpad.net/python-mode

Installing new modules

Although many applications and modules have searchable webpages, there is a central repository [1] for searching packages for installation, known as the "Cheese Shop."

See Also

- EasyInstall [2]

Previous: Getting Python	Index	Next: Interactive mode

References

[1] http://www.python.org/pypi
[2] http://peak.telecommunity.com/DevCenter/EasyInstall

Python Programming/Interactive mode

| Previous: Setting it up | Index | Next: Self Help |

Python has two basic modes: The normal "mode" is the mode where the scripted and finished .py files are run in the python interpreter. Interactive mode is a command line shell which gives immediate feedback for each statement, while running previously fed statements in active memory. As new lines are fed into the interpreter, the fed program is evaluated both in part and in whole.

To get into interactive mode, simply type "python" without any arguments. This is a good way to play around and try variations on syntax. Python should print something like this:

```
$ python
Python 3.0b3 (r30b3:66303, Sep  8 2008, 14:01:02) [MSC v.1500 32 bit (Intel)] on win32
Type "help", "copyright", "credits" or "license" for more information.
>>>
```

(If Python doesn't run, make sure your path is set correctly. See Getting Python.)

The >>> is Python's way of telling you that you are in interactive mode. In interactive mode what you type is immediately run. Try typing 1+1 in. Python will respond with 2. Interactive mode allows you to test out and see what Python will do. If you ever feel the need to play with new Python statements, go into interactive mode and try them out.

A sample interactive session:

```
>>> 5
5
>>> print (5*7)
35
>>> "hello" * 4
'hellohellohellohello'
>>> "hello".__class__
<type 'str'>
```

However, you need to be careful in the interactive environment to avoid any confusion. For example, the following is a valid Python script:

```
if 1:
  print("True")
print("Done")
```

If you try to enter this as written in the interactive environment, you might be surprised by the result:

```
>>> if 1:
...     print("True")
... print("Done")
  File "<stdin>", line 3
    print("Done")
        ^
SyntaxError: invalid syntax
```

What the interpreter is saying is that the indentation of the second print was unexpected. What you should have entered was a blank line to end the first (i.e., "if") statement, before you started writing the next print statement. For example, you should have entered the statements as though they were written:

```
if 1:
   print("True")

print("Done")
```

Which would have resulted in the following:

```
>>> if 1:
...     print("True")
...
True
>>> print("Done")
Done
>>>
```

Interactive mode

Instead of Python exiting when the program is finished, you can use the -i flag to start an interactive session. This can be **very** useful for debugging and prototyping.

```
python -i hello.py
```

| Previous: Setting it up | Index | Next: Self Help |

Python Programming/Self Help

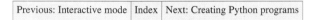

This book is useful for learning python, but indeed there might be topics that the book does not cover. You might want to search for modules in the standard library, or perhaps inspecting an unknown object's functions, or perhaps you know there is a function that you have to call inside an object but you don't know its name. That's where the interactive help() comes to play.

Navigating help

When you enter the help system through the `help()` call within the interactive session, you are presented with a quick introduction to the help system. "Welcome to Python 2.6! This is the online help utility.

If this is your first time using Python, you should definitely check out the tutorial on the Internet at http://docs.python.org/tutorial/".

You can access the different portions of help simply by typing in `modules`, `keywords`, or `topics`.

Typing in the name of one of these will print the help page associated with the item in question. To get a list of available modules, keywords, or topics, type "modules","keywords", or "topics". Each module also comes with a one-line summary of what it does; to list the modules whose summaries contain a given word such as "spam", type "modules spam".

You can exit the help system by typing "quit" or by entering a blank line to return to the interpreter.

Help parameter

You can obtain information on a specific command without entering interactive help. For example, you can obtain help on a given topic simply by adding a string in quotes, such as `help("object")`. You may also obtain help on a given object as well, by passing it as a parameter to the help function.

| Previous: Interactive mode | Index | Next: Creating Python programs |

Python Programming/Creating Python programs

Previous: Self Help	Index	Next: Variables and Strings

Welcome to Python! This tutorial will show you how to start writing programs.

Python programs are nothing more than text files, and they may be edited with a standard text editor program.[1] What text editor you use will probably depend on your operating system: any text editor can create Python programs. It is easier to use a text editor that includes Python syntax highlighting, however.

Hello, World!

The first program that every programmer writes is called the "Hello, World!" program. This program simply outputs the phrase "Hello, World!" and then quits. Let's write "Hello, World!" in Python!

Open up your text editor and create a new file called hello.py containing just this line (you can copy-paste if you want):

```
print("Hello, world!")
```

This program uses the print function, which simply outputs its parameters to the terminal. print ends with a newline character, which simply moves the cursor to the next line.

Now that you've written your first program, let's run it in Python! This process differs slightly depending on your operating system.

Windows

- Create a folder on your computer to use for your Python programs, such as C:\pythonpractice, and save your hello.py program in that folder.
- In the Start menu, select "Run...", and type in cmd. This will cause the Windows terminal to open.
- Type cd \pythonpractice to **c**hange **d**irectory to your pythonpractice folder, and hit Enter.
- Type python hello.py to run your program!

If it didn't work, make sure your PATH contains the python directory. See Getting Python.

Mac

- Create a folder on your computer to use for your Python programs. A good suggestion would be to name it pythonpractice and place it in your Home folder (the one that contains folders for Documents, Movies, Music, Pictures, etc). Save your hello.py program into this folder.
- Open the Applications folder, go into the Utilities folder, and open the Terminal program.
- Type cd pythonpractice to **c**hange **d**irectory to your pythonpractice folder, and hit Enter.
- Type python hello.py to run your program!

<span class="citation wikicite" id="endnote_If you have both python version 2.6.1 and version 3.0 installed(Very possible if you are using Ubuntu, and ran **sudo apt-get python3** to have python3 installed), you should run python3 hello.py">^

Linux

- Create a folder on your computer to use for your Python programs, such as ~/pythonpractice, and save your hello.py program in that folder.
- Open up the terminal program. In KDE, open the main menu and select "Run Command..." to open Konsole. In GNOME, open the main menu, open the Applications folder, open the Accessories folder, and select Terminal.
- Type cd ~/pythonpractice to change directory to your pythonpractice folder, and hit Enter.
- Type python hello.py to run your program!

Result

The program should print:

```
Hello, world!
```

Congratulations! You're well on your way to becoming a Python programmer.

Exercises

1. Modify the hello.py program to say hello to a historical political leader (or to Ada Lovelace).
2. Change the program so that after the greeting, it asks, "How did you get here?".
3. Re-write the original program to use two print statements: one for "Hello" and one for "world". The program should still only print out on one line.

Solutions

Notes

[1] Sometimes, Python programs are distributed in compiled form. We won't have to worry about that for quite a while.

Previous: Self Help	Index	Next: Variables and Strings

Python Programming/Basic Math

Previous: Variables and Strings	Index	Next: Decision Control

Now that we know how to work with numbers and strings, let's write a program that might actually be useful! Let's say you want to find out how much you weigh in stone. A concise program can make short work of this task. Since a stone is 14 pounds, and there are about 2.2 pounds in a kilogram, the following formula should do the trick:

$$m_{stone} = \frac{m_{kg} \times 2.2}{14}$$

So, let's turn this formula into a program!

```
mass_kg = int(raw_input("What is your mass in kilograms?" ))
mass_stone = mass_kg * 2.2 / 14
print("You weigh", mass_stone, "stone.")
```

Run this program and get your weight in stone! Notice that applying the formula was as simple as putting in a few mathematical statements:

```
mass_stone = mass_kg * 2.2 / 14
```

Mathematical Operators

Here are some commonly used mathematical operators

Syntax	Math	Operation Name
a+b	$a + b$	addition
a-b	$a - b$	subtraction
a*b	$a \times b$	multiplication
a/b	$a \div b$	division (see note below)
a//b	$a \div b$	floor division (e.g. 5/2=2) - Available in Python 2.2 and later
a%b	$a \bmod b$	modulo
-a	$-a$	negation
abs(a)	$\|a\|$	absolute value
a**b	a^b	exponent
math.sqrt(a)	$\sqrt{a}$	square root

Beware that due to the limitations of floating point arithmetic, rounding errors can cause unexpected results. For example:

```
>>> print(0.6/0.2)
3.0
>>> print(0.6//0.2)
2.0
```

For the Python 2.x series / does "floor division" for integers and longs (e.g. 5/2=2) but "true division" for floats and complex (e.g. 5.0/2.0=2.5). For Python 3.x, / does "true division" for all types.[1] [2]

Order of Operations

Python uses the standard order of operations as taught in Algebra and Geometry classes at high school or secondary school. That is, mathematical expressions are evaluated in the following order (memorized by many as PEMDAS), which is also applied to parentheticals.

(Note that operations which share a table row are performed from left to right. That is, a division to the left of a multiplication, with no parentheses between them, is performed before the multiplication simply because it is to the left.)

Name	Syntax	Description	PEMDAS Mnemonic
Parentheses	(...)	Before operating on anything else, Python must evaluate all parentheticals starting at the innermost level. (This includes functions.)	Please
Exponents	**	As an exponent is simply short multiplication or division, it should be evaluated before them.	Excuse
Multiplication and Division	* / // %	Again, multiplication is rapid addition and must, therefore, happen first.	My Dear
Addition and Subtraction	+ -		Aunt Sally

Formatting output

Wouldn't it be nice if we always worked with nice round numbers while doing math? Unfortunately, the real world is not quite so neat and tidy as we would like it to be. Sometimes, we end up with long, ugly numbers like the following:

```
What is your mass in kilograms? 65
You weigh 10.2142857143 stone.
```

By default, Python's print statement prints numbers to 10 significant figures. But what if you only want one or two? We can use the round() function, which rounds a number to the number of decimal points you choose. round() takes two arguments: the number you want to round, and the number of decimal places to round it to. For example:

```
>>> print (round(3.14159265, 2))
3.14
```

Now, let's change our program to only print the result to two significant figures.

```
print ("You weigh", round(mass_stone, 2), "stone.")
```

This also demonstrates the concept of nesting functions. As you can see, you can place one function inside another function, and everything will still work exactly the way you would expect. If you don't like this, you can always use multiple variables, instead:

```
twoSigFigs = round(mass_stone, 2)
numToString = str(twoSigFigs)
print ("You weigh " + numToString + " stone.")
```

Exercises

1. Ask the user to specify the number of sides on a polygon and find the number of diagonals [3] within the polygon.
2. Take the lengths of two sides to a triangle from the user and apply the Pythagorean Theorem to find the third.

Notes

[1] What's New in Python 2.2 (http://www.python.org/doc/2.2.3/whatsnew/node7.html)
[2] PEP 238 -- Changing the Division Operator (http://www.python.org/dev/peps/pep-0238/)
[3] http://www.mathopenref.com/polygondiagonal.html

Previous: Variables and Strings	Index	Next: Decision Control

Python Programming/Decision Control

Previous: Sequences	Index	Next: Conditional Statements

Python, like many other computer programming languages, uses Boolean logic for its decision control. That is, the Python interpreter compares one or more values in order to decide whether to execute a piece of code or not, given the proper syntax and instructions.

Decision control is then divided into two major categories, conditional and repetition. Conditional logic simply uses the keyword **if** and a Boolean expression to decide whether or not to execute a code block. Repetition builds on the conditional constructs by giving us a simple method in which to repeat a block of code while a Boolean expression evaluates to *true*.

Boolean Expressions

Here is a little example of boolean expressions (you don't have to type it in):

```
a = 6
b = 7
c = 42
print (1, a == 6)
print (2, a == 7)
print (3, a == 6 and b == 7)
print (4, a == 7 and b == 7)
print (5, not a == 7 and b == 7)
print (6, a == 7 or b == 7)
print (7, a == 7 or b == 6)
print (8, not (a == 7 and b == 6))
print (9, not a == 7 and b == 6)
```

With the output being:

```
1 True
2 False
3 True
4 False
```

```
5 True
6 True
7 False
8 True
9 False
```

What is going on? The program consists of a bunch of funny looking `print` statements. Each `print` statement prints a number and an expression. The number is to help keep track of which statement I am dealing with. Notice how each expression ends up being either True or False; these are built-in Python values.

The lines:

```
print (1, a == 6)
print (2, a == 7)
```

print out True and False respectively, just as expected, since the first is true and the second is false. The third print, `print (3, a == 6 and b == 7)`, is a little different. The operator `and` means if both the statement before and the statement after are true then the whole expression is true otherwise the whole expression is false. The next line, `print (4, a == 7 and b == 7)`, shows how if part of an `and` expression is false, the whole thing is false. The behavior of `and` can be summarized as follows:

expression	result
true and true	true
true and false	false
false and true	false
false and false	false

Note that if the first expression is false Python does not check the second expression since it knows the whole expression is false.

The next line, `print (5, not a == 7 and b == 7)`, uses the `not` operator. `not` just gives the opposite of the expression (The expression could be rewritten as `print (5, a != 7 and b == 7)`). Here's the table:

expression	result
not true	false
not false	true

The two following lines, `print (6, a == 7 or b == 7)` and `print (7, a == 7 or b == 6)`, use the `or` operator. The `or` operator returns true if the first expression is true, or if the second expression is true or both are true. If neither are true it returns false. Here's the table:

expression	result
true or true	true
true or false	true
false or true	true
false or false	false

Note that if the first expression is true Python doesn't check the second expression since it knows the whole expression is true. This works since or is true if at least one half of the expression is true. The first part is true so the second part could be either false or true, but the whole expression is still true.

The next two lines, print (8, not (a == 7 and b == 6)) and print (9, not a == 7 and b == 6), show that parentheses can be used to group expressions and force one part to be evaluated first. Notice that the parentheses changed the expression from false to true. This occurred since the parentheses forced the not to apply to the whole expression instead of just the a == 7 portion.

Here is an example of using a boolean expression:

```
list = ["Life","The Universe","Everything","Jack","Jill","Life","Jill"]

# Make a copy of the list.
copy = list[:]
# Sort the copy
copy.sort()
prev = copy[0]
del copy[0]


count = 0

# Go through the list searching for a match
while count < len(copy) and copy[count] != prev:
    prev = copy[count]
    count = count + 1

# If a match was not found then count can't be < len
# since the while loop continues while count is < len
# and no match is found
if count < len(copy):
    print ("First Match:",prev)
```

See the Lists chapter to explain what [:] means on the first line.

Here is the output:

```
First Match: Jill
```

This program works by continuing to check for match while count < len(copy) and copy[count]. When either count is greater than the last index of copy or a match has been found the and is no longer true so the loop exits. The if simply checks to make sure that the while exited because a match was found.

The other 'trick' of and is used in this example. If you look at the table for and notice that the third entry is "false and won't check". If count >= len(copy) (in other words count < len(copy) is false) then copy[count] is never looked at. This is because Python knows that if the first is false then they both can't be true. This is known as a short circuit and is useful if the second half of the `and` will cause an error if something is wrong. I used the first expression (`count < len(copy)`) to check and see if `count` was a valid index for `copy`. (If you don't believe me remove the matches `Jill' and `Life', check that it still works and then reverse the order of `count < len(copy) and copy[count] != prev` to `copy[count] != prev and count < len(copy)`.)

Boolean expressions can be used when you need to check two or more different things at once.

Examples

password1.py

```
## This programs asks a user for a name and a password.
# It then checks them to make sure that the user is allowed in.
# Note that this is a simple and insecure example,
# real password code should never be implemented this way.

name = raw_input("What is your name? ")
password = raw_input("What is the password? ")
if name == "Josh" and password == "Friday":
    print ("Welcome Josh")
elif name == "Fred" and password == "Rock":
    print ("Welcome Fred")
else:
    print ("I don't know you.")
```

Sample runs

```
What is your name? Josh
What is the password? Friday
Welcome Josh

What is your name? Bill
What is the password? Saturday
I don't know you.
```

Exercises

1. Write a program that has a user guess your name, but they only get 3 chances to do so until the program quits.

Solutions

Previous: Sequences	Index	Next: Conditional Statements

Python Programming/Conditional Statements

| Previous: Decision Control | Index | Next: Loops |

Decisions

A **Decision** is when a program has more than one choice of actions depending on a variable's value. Think of a traffic light. When it is green, we continue our drive. When we see the light turn yellow, we proceed to reduce our speed, and when it is red, we stop. These are logical decisions that depend on the value of the traffic light. Luckily, Python has a decision statement to help us when our application needs to make such decision for the user.

If statement

Here is a warm-up exercise - a short program to compute the absolute value of a number:

```
n = raw_input("Integer? ")#Pick an integer.  And remember, if raw_input
 is not supported by your OS, use input()
n = int(n)#Defines n as the integer you chose. (Alternatively, you can
define n yourself)
if n < 0:
    print ("The absolute value of",n,"is",-n)
else:
    print ("The absolute value of",n,"is",n)
```

Here is the output from the two times that I ran this program:

```
Integer? -34
The absolute value of -34 is 34

Integer? 1
The absolute value of 1 is 1
```

What does the computer do when it sees this piece of code? First it prompts the user for a number with the statement "n = raw_input("Integer? ")". Next it reads the line "if n < 0:". If n is less than zero Python runs the line "print "The absolute value of",n,"is",-n". Otherwise python runs the line "print "The absolute value of",n,"is",n".

More formally, Python looks at whether the *expression* n < 0 is true or false. An if statement is followed by an indented *block* of statements that are run when the expression is true. After the if statement is an optional else statement and another indented *block* of statements. This 2nd block of statements is run if the expression is false.

Expressions can be tested several different ways. Here is a table of all of them:

operator	function
<	less than
<=	less than or equal to
>	greater than
>=	greater than or equal to
==	equal
!=	not equal

Another feature of the `if` command is the `elif` statement. It stands for "else if," which means that if the original `if` statement is false and the `elif` statement is true, execute the block of code following the `elif` statement. Here's an example:

```
a = 0
while a < 10:
    a = a + 1
    if a > 5:
        print (a,">",5)
    elif a <= 7:
        print (a,"<=",7)
    else:
        print ("Neither test was true")
```

and the output:

```
1 <= 7
2 <= 7
3 <= 7
4 <= 7
5 <= 7
6 > 5
7 > 5
8 > 5
9 > 5
10 > 5
```

Notice how the `elif a <= 7` is only tested when the `if` statement fails to be true. `elif` allows multiple tests to be done in a single if statement.

If Examples

High_low.py

```
#Plays the guessing game higher or lower
# (originally written by Josh Cogliati, improved by Quique)

#This should actually be something that is semi random like the
# last digits of the time or something else, but that will have to
# wait till a later chapter.  (Extra Credit, modify it to be random
```

```
# after the Modules chapter)

#This is for demonstration purposes only.
# It is not written to handle invalid input like a full program would.
number = 78
guess = 0

while guess != number :
    guess = raw_input("Guess an integer: ")
    guess = int(guess)
    if guess > number :
        print ("Too high")

    elif guess < number :
        print ("Too low")
    else:
        print ("Just right" )
```

Sample run:

```
Guess an integer:100
Too high
Guess an integer:50
Too low
Guess an integer:75
Too low
Guess an integer:87
Too high
Guess an integer:81
Too high
Guess an integer:78
Just right
```

even.py

```
#Asks for a number.
#Prints if it is even or odd

number = raw_input("Tell me a number: ")
number = float(number)
if number % 2 == 0:
    print (number,"is even.")
elif number % 2 == 1:
    print (number,"is odd.")
else:
    print (number,"is very strange.")
```

Sample runs.

```
Tell me a number: 3
3 is odd.

Tell me a number: 2
2 is even.

Tell me a number: 3.14159
3.14159 is very strange.
```

average1.py

```
#keeps asking for numbers until 0 is entered.
#Prints the average value.

count = 0
sum = 0.0
number = 1.0  # set this to something that will not exit
#                the while loop immediately.

print ("Enter 0 to exit the loop")

while number != 0:
    number = raw_input("Enter a number: ")
    number = float(number)
    if number != 0:
        count = count + 1
        sum = sum + number

print "The average was:",sum/count
```

Sample runs

```
Enter 0 to exit the loop
Enter a number:3
Enter a number:5
Enter a number:0
The average was: 4.0

Enter 0 to exit the loop
Enter a number:1
Enter a number:4
Enter a number:3
Enter a number:0
The average was: 2.66666666667
```

average2.py

```
#keeps asking for numbers until count have been entered.
#Prints the average value.
```

```
sum = 0.0

print ("This program will take several numbers, then average them.")
count = raw_input("How many numbers would you like to sum:")
count = int(count)
current_count = 0

while current_count < count:
    current_count = current_count + 1
    print ("Number",current_count)
    number = input("Enter a number: ")
    sum = sum + number

print "The average was:",sum/count
```

Sample runs

```
This program will take several numbers, then average them.
How many numbers would you like to sum:2
Number 1
Enter a number:3
Number 2
Enter a number:5
The average was: 4.0


This program will take several numbers, then average them.
How many numbers would you like to sum:3
Number 1
Enter a number:1
Number 2
Enter a number:4
Number 3
Enter a number:3
The average was: 2.66666666667
```

If Exercises

1. Write a password guessing program to keep track of how many times the user has entered the password wrong. If it is more than 3 times, print *You have been denied access.* and terminate the program. If the password is correct, print *You have successfully logged in.* and terminate the program.
2. Write a program that asks for two numbers. If the sum of the numbers is greater than 100, print *That is a big number* and terminate the program.
3. Write a program that asks the user their name. If they enter your name, say "That is a nice name." If they enter "John Cleese" or "Michael Palin", tell them how you feel about them ;), otherwise tell them "You have a nice name."

Conditional Statements

Many languages (like Java and PHP) have the concept of a one-line conditional (called The Ternary Operator), often used to simplify conditionally accessing a value. For instance (in Java):

```
int in= ; // read from program input

// a normal conditional assignment
int res;
if(in < 0)
  res = -in;
else
  res = in;

// this can be simplified to
int res2 = (in < 0) ? -in: in;
```

For many years Python did not have the same construct natively, however you could replicate it by constructing a tuple of results and calling the test as the index of the tuple, like so:

```
in = int(raw_input("Enter a number to get its absolute value:"))
res = (-in,in)[in<0]
```

It is important to note that, unlike a built in conditional statement, both the true and false branches are evaluated before returning, which can lead to unexpected results and slower executions if you're not careful. To resolve this issue, and as a better practice, wrap whatever you put in the tuple in anonymous function calls (lambda notation) to prevent them from being evaluated until the desired branch is called:

```
in = int(raw_input("Enter a number to get its absolute value:"))
res = (lambda:in,lambda:-in)[in<0]()
```

Since Python 2.5 however, there has been an equivalent operator to The Ternary Operator (though not called such, and with a totally different syntax):

```
in = int(raw_input("Enter a number to get its absolute value:"))
res = -in if in<0 else in
```

Switch

A switch is a control statement present in most computer programming languages to minimize a bunch of If - elif statements. Sadly Python doesn't officially support this statement, but with the clever use of an array or dictionary, we can recreate this Switch statement that depends on a value.

```
x = 1

def hello():
  print ("Hello")

def bye():
  print ("Bye")

def hola():
  print ("Hola is Spanish for Hello")
```

```
def adios():
  print ("Adios is Spanish for Bye")

# Notice that our switch statement is a regular variable, only that we
added the function's name inside
# and there are no quotes
menu = [hello,bye,hola,adios]

# To call our switch statement, we simply make reference to the array
with a pair of parentheses
# at the end to call the function
menu[3]()    # calls the adios function since is number 3 in our array.

menu[0]()    # Calls the hello function being our first element in our
array.

menu[x]()    # Calls the bye function as is the second element on the
array x = 1
```

This works because Python stores a reference of the function in the array at its particular index, and by adding a pair of parentheses we are actually calling the function. Here the last line is equivalent to:

```
if x==0:
    hello()
elif x==1:
    bye()
elif x==2:
    hola()
else:
    adios()
```

Another way

Source [1]

Another way is to use lambdas. Code pasted here without permissions.

```
result = {
  'a': lambda x: x * 5,
  'b': lambda x: x + 7,
  'c': lambda x: x - 2
}[value](x)
```

| Previous: Decision Control | Index | Next: Loops |

References

[1] http://simonwillison.net/2004/May/7/switch/

Python Programming/Loops

Previous: Conditional Statements	Index	Next: Sequences

While loops

This is our first control structure. Ordinarily the computer starts with the first line and then goes down from there. Control structures change the order that statements are executed or decide if a certain statement will be run. As a side note, decision statements (e.g., if statements) also influence whether or not a certain statement will run. Here's the source for a program that uses the while control structure:

```
a = 0
while a < 10 :
    a += 1
    print (a)
```

And here is the output:

```
1
2
3
4
5
6
7
8
9
10
```

So what does the program do? First it sees the line `a = 0` and makes a zero. Then it sees `while a < 10:` and so the computer checks to see if `a < 10`. The first time the computer sees this statement a is zero so it is less than 10. In other words while a is less than ten the computer will run the tabbed in statements.

Here is another example of the use of `while`:

```
a = 1
s = 0
print ('Enter Numbers to add to the sum.')
print ('Enter 0 to quit.')
while a != 0:
    print ('Current Sum: ', s)
    a = raw_input ('Number? ')
    a = float(a)
    s += a
print ('Total Sum = ',s)
```

Python Programming/Loops 24

```
Enter Numbers to add to the sum.
Enter 0 to quit.
Current Sum: 0
Number? 200
Current Sum: 200
Number? -15.25
Current Sum: 184.75
Number? -151.85
Current Sum: 32.9
Number? 10.00
Current Sum: 42.9
Number? 0
Total Sum = 42.9
```

Notice how `print 'Total Sum =',s` is only run at the end. The `while` statement only affects the lines that are tabbed in (a.k.a. indented). The `!=` means does not equal so `while a != 0 :` means until a is zero run the tabbed in statements that are afterwards.

Now that we have while loops, it is possible to have programs that run forever. An easy way to do this is to write a program like this:

```
while 1 == 1:
    print ("Help, I'm stuck in a loop.")
```

This program will output `Help, I'm stuck in a loop.` until the heat death of the universe or you stop it. The way to stop it is to hit the Control (or Ctrl) button and `c' (the letter) at the same time. This will kill the program. (Note: sometimes you will have to hit enter after the Control C.)

Examples

Fibonacci.py

```
#This program calculates the Fibonacci sequence
a = 0
b = 1
count = 0
max_count = 20
while count < max_count:
    count = count + 1
    #we need to keep track of a since we change it
    old_a = a
    old_b = b
    a = old_b
    b = old_a + old_b
    #Notice that the , at the end of a print statement keeps it
    # from switching to a new line
    print (old_a,)
print ()
```

Output:

```
0 1 1 2 3 5 8 13 21 34 55 89 144 233 377 610 987 1597 2584 4181
```

Password.py

```
# Waits until a password has been entered.  Use control-C to break out
without
# the password

# Note that this must not be the password so that the
# while loop runs at least once.
password = "foobar"

#note that != means not equal
while password != "unicorn":
    password = raw_input("Password: ")
print ("Welcome in")
```

Sample run:

```
Password:auo
Password:y22
Password:password
Password:open sesame
Password:unicorn
Welcome in
```

For Loops

This is another way of using loops:

```
onetoten = range(1,11)
for count in onetoten:
    print (count)
```

The output:

```
1
2
3
4
5
6
7
8
9
10
```

The output looks very familiar, but the program code looks different. The first line uses the range function. The range function uses two arguments like this range(start,finish). start is the first number that is produced. finish is one larger than the last number. Note that this program could have been done in a shorter way:

```
for count in range(1,11):
    print (count)
```

Here are some examples to show what happens with the `range` command:

```
>>> range(1,10)
[1, 2, 3, 4, 5, 6, 7, 8, 9]
>>> range(-32, -20)
[-32, -31, -30, -29, -28, -27, -26, -25, -24, -23, -22, -21]
>>> range(5,21)
[5, 6, 7, 8, 9, 10, 11, 12, 13, 14, 15, 16, 17, 18, 19, 20]
>>> range(21,5)
[]
```

Another way to use the `range()` function in a `for` loop is to supply only one argument:

```
for a in range(10):
    print a,
```

The above code acts exactly the same as:

```
for a in range(0, 10):
    print a,
```

with 0 implied as the starting point. The output is

```
0 1 2 3 4 5 6 7 8 9
```

The code would cycle through the `for` loop 10 times as expected, but starting with 0 instead of 1.

The next line `for count in onetoten:` uses the `for` control structure. A `for` control structure looks like `for variable in list:`. `list` is gone through starting with the first element of the list and going to the last. As `for` goes through each element in a list it puts each into `variable`. That allows `variable` to be used in each successive time the for loop is run through. Here is another example to demonstrate:

```
demolist = ['life',42, 'the universe', 6,'and',7,'everything']
for item in demolist:
    print ("The Current item is: %s" % item)
```

The output is:

```
The Current item is: life
The Current item is: 42
The Current item is: the universe
The Current item is: 6
The Current item is: and
The Current item is: 7
The Current item is: everything
```

Notice how the for loop goes through and sets item to each element in the list. (Notice how if you don't want `print` to go to the next line add a comma at the end of the statement (i.e. if you want to print something else on that line).) So, what is `for` good for? The first use is to go through all the elements of a list and do something with each of them. Here a quick way to add up all the elements:

```
list = [2,4,6,8]
sum = 0
for num in list:
    sum = sum + num
```

```
print "The sum is: %d" % sum
```

with the output simply being:

```
The sum is:   20
```

Or you could write a program to find out if there are any duplicates in a list like this program does:

```
list = [4, 5, 7, 8, 9, 1,0,7,10]
list.sort()
prev = list[0]
del list[0]
for item in list:
    if prev == item:
        print ("Duplicate of ",prev," Found")
    prev = item
```

and for good measure:

```
Duplicate of   7   Found
```

How does it work? Here is a special debugging version:

```
l = [4, 5, 7, 8, 9, 1,0,7,10]
print ("l = [4, 5, 7, 8, 9, 1,0,7,10]","\tl:",l)
l.sort()
print ("l.sort()","\tl:",l)
prev = l[0]
print ("prev = l[0]","\tprev:",prev)
del l[0]
print ("del l[0]","\tl:",l)
for item in l:
    if prev == item:
        print ("Duplicate of ",prev," Found")
    print ("if prev == item:","\tprev:",prev,"\titem:",item)
    prev = item
    print ("prev = item","\t\tprev:",prev,"\titem:",item)
```

with the output being:

```
l = [4, 5, 7, 8, 9, 1,0,7,10]    l: [4, 5, 7, 8, 9, 1, 0, 7, 10]
l.sort()          l: [0, 1, 4, 5, 7, 7, 8, 9, 10]
prev = l[0]      prev: 0
del l[0]          l: [1, 4, 5, 7, 7, 8, 9, 10]
if prev == item:        prev: 0          item: 1
prev = item            prev: 1          item: 1
if prev == item:        prev: 1          item: 4
prev = item            prev: 4          item: 4
if prev == item:        prev: 4          item: 5
prev = item            prev: 5          item: 5
if prev == item:        prev: 5          item: 7
prev = item            prev: 7          item: 7
```

```
Duplicate of  7  Found
if prev == item:          prev: 7          item: 7
prev = item               prev: 7          item: 7
if prev == item:          prev: 7          item: 8
prev = item               prev: 8          item: 8
if prev == item:          prev: 8          item: 9
prev = item               prev: 9          item: 9
if prev == item:          prev: 9          item: 10
prev = item               prev: 10         item: 10
```

Note: The reason there are so many `print` statements is because print statements can show the value of each variable at different times, and help debug the program. First the program starts with a old list. Next the program sorts the list. This is so that any duplicates get put next to each other. The program then initializes a prev(ious) variable. Next the first element of the list is deleted so that the first item is not incorrectly thought to be a duplicate. Next a for loop is gone into. Each item of the list is checked to see if it is the same as the previous. If it is a duplicate was found. The value of prev is then changed so that the next time the for loop is run through prev is the previous item to the current. Sure enough, the 7 is found to be a duplicate.

The other way to use for loops is to do something a certain number of times. Here is some code to print out the first 9 numbers of the Fibonacci series:

```
a = 1
b = 1
for c in range(1,10):
    print (a)
    n = a + b
    a = b
    b = n
print ("")
```

with the surprising output:

```
1
1
2
3
5
8
13
21
34
```

Everything that can be done with `for` loops can also be done with `while` loops but `for` loops give a easy way to go through all the elements in a list or to do something a certain number of times.

Exercises

1. Create a program to count by prime numbers. Ask the user to input a number, then print each prime number up to that number.
2. Instruct the user to pick an arbitrary number from 1 to 100 and proceed to guess it correctly within seven tries. After each guess, the user must tell whether their number is higher than, lower than, or equal to your guess.

Solutions

Previous: Conditional Statements	Index	Next: Sequences

Python Programming/Sequences

Previous: Basic Math	Index	Next: Source Documentation and Comments

Sequences allow you to store multiple values in an organized and efficient fashion. There are five kinds of sequences in Python: strings, lists, tuples, dictionaries, and sets (actually there are more, but these are the most commonly used types).

Strings

We already covered strings, but that was before you knew what a sequence is. In other languages, the elements in arrays and sometimes the characters in strings may be accessed with the square brackets, or subscript operator. This works in Python too:

```
>>> "Hello, world!"[0]
'H'
>>> "Hello, world!"[1]
'e'
>>> "Hello, world!"[2]
'l'
>>> "Hello, world!"[3]
'l'
>>> "Hello, world!"[4]
'o'
```

Indexes are numbered from 0 to n-1 where n is the number of items (or characters), and they are positioned between the items:

```
 H  e  l  l  o  ,  _  w  o  r  l  d  !
 0  1  2  3  4  5  6  7  8  9 10 11 12
```

The item which comes immediately after an index is the one selected by that index. Negative indexes are counted from the end of the string:

```
>>> "Hello, world!"[-2]
'd'
>>> "Hello, world!"[-9]
'o'
```

```
>>> "Hello, world!"[-13]
'H'
>>> "Hello, world!"[-1]
'!'
```

But in Python, the colon : allows the square brackets to take as many as two numbers. For any sequence which only uses numeric indexes, this will return the portion which is between the specified indexes. This is known as "slicing," and the result of slicing a string is often called a "substring."

```
>>> "Hello, world!"[3:9]
'lo, wo'
>>> string = "Hello, world!"
>>> string[:5]
'Hello'
>>> string[-6:-1]
'world'
>>> string[-9:]
'o, world!'
>>> string[:-8]
'Hello'
>>> string[:]
'Hello, world!'
```

As demonstrated above, if either number is omitted it is assumed to be the beginning or end of the sequence.

Lists

A list is just what it sounds like: a list of values, organized in order. A list is created using square brackets. For example, an empty list would be initialized like this:

```
spam = []
```

The values of the list are separated by commas. For example:

```
spam = ["bacon", "eggs", 42]
```

Lists may contain objects of varying types. It may hold both the strings "eggs" and "bacon" as well as the number 42.

Like characters in a string, items in a list can be accessed by indexes starting at 0. To access a specific item in a list, you refer to it by the name of the list, followed by the item's number in the list inside brackets. For example:

```
>>> spam
['bacon', 'eggs', 42]
>>> spam[0]
'bacon'
>>> spam[1]
'eggs'
>>> spam[2]
42
```

You can also use negative numbers, which count backwards from the end of the list:

```
>>> spam[-1]
42
```

```
>>> spam[-2]
'eggs'
>>> spam[-3]
'bacon'
```

The len() function also works on lists, returning the number of items in the array:

```
>>> len(spam)
3
```

Note that the len() function counts the number of item inside a list, so the last item in spam (42) has the index (len(spam) - 1).

The items in a list can also be changed, just like the contents of an ordinary variable:

```
>>> spam = ["bacon", "eggs", 42]
>>> spam
['bacon', 'eggs', 42]
>>> spam[1]
'eggs'
>>> spam[1] = "ketchup"
>>> spam
['bacon', 'ketchup', 42]
```

(Strings, being *immutable*, are impossible to modify.) As with strings, lists may be sliced:

```
>>> spam[1:]
['eggs', 42]
>>> spam[:-1]
[42]
```

It is also possible to add items to a list. There are many ways to do it, the easiest way is to use the append() method of list:

```
>>> spam.append(10)
>>> spam
['bacon', 'eggs', 42, 10]
```

Note that you cannot manually insert an element by specifying the index outside of its range. The following code would fail:

```
>>> spam[4] = 10
IndexError: list assignment index out of range
```

Instead, you must use the append() function. If you want to insert an item inside a list at a certain index, you may use the insert() method of list, for example:

```
>>> spam.insert(1, 'and')
>>> spam
['bacon', 'and', 'eggs', 42, 10]
```

You can also delete items from a list using the del statement:

```
>>> spam
['bacon', 'and', 'eggs', 42, 10]
```

```
>>> del spam[1]
>>> spam
['bacon', 'eggs', 42, 10]
>>> spam[0]
'bacon'
>>> spam[1]
'eggs'
>>> spam[2]
42
>>> spam[3]
10
```

As you can see, the list re-orders itself, so there are no gaps in the numbering.

For further explanation on list, see Data Structure/Lists

Tuples

Tuples are similar to lists, except they are immutable. Once you have set a tuple, there is no way to change it whatsoever: you cannot add, change, or remove elements of a tuple. Otherwise, tuples work identically to lists.

To declare a tuple, you use commas:

```
unchanging = "rocks", 0, "the universe"
```

It is often necessary to use parentheses to differentiate between different tuples, such as when doing multiple assignments on the same line:

```
foo, bar = "rocks", 0, "the universe" # An error: 2 elements on left, 3
 on right
foo, bar = "rocks", (0, "the universe")
```

Unnecessary parenthesis can be used without harm, but nested parentheses denote nested tuples:

```
>>> var = "me", "you", "us", "them"
>>> var = ("me", "you", "us", "them")
```

both produce:

```
>>> print var
('me', 'you', 'us', 'them')
```

but:

```
>>> var = ("me", "you", ("us", "them"))
>>> print(var)
('me', 'you', ('us', 'them')) # A tuple of 3 elements, the last of
which is itself a tuple.
```

For further explanation on tuple, see *Data Structure/Tuples*

Dictionaries

Dictionaries are also like lists, and they are mutable -- you can add, change, and remove elements from a dictionary. However, the elements in a dictionary are not bound to numbers, the way a list is. Every element in a dictionary has two parts: a key, and a value. Calling a key of a dictionary returns the value linked to that key. You could consider a list to be a special kind of dictionary, in which the key of every element is a number, in numerical order.

Dictionaries are declared using curly braces, and each element is declared first by its key, then a colon, and then its value. For example:

```
>>> definitions = {"guava": "a tropical fruit", "python": "a programming
language", "the answer": 42}
>>> definitions
{'python': 'a programming language', 'the answer': 42, 'guava': 'a
tropical fruit'}
>>> definitions["the answer"]
42
>>> definitions["guava"]
'a tropical fruit'
>>> len(definitions)
3
```

Also, adding an element to a dictionary is much simpler: simply declare it as you would a variable.

```
>>> definitions["new key"] = "new value"
>>> definitions
{'python': 'a programming language', 'the answer': 42, 'guava': 'a
tropical fruit', 'new key': 'new value'}
```

For further explanation on dictionary, see *Data Structure/Dictionaries*

Sets

Sets are just like list, except that it is **unordered** and it does not allow duplicate values. Elements of a set are neither bound to a number (like list and tuple) nor to a key (like dictionary). The reason for using set over other data types is that set is much faster for huge number of items than a list or tuple and sets provide fast data insertion, deletion, and fast membership testing. Sets also support mathematical set operations such as testing for subsets and finding the union or intersection of two sets.

```
>>> mind = set([42, 'a string', (23, 4)])
>>> mind
set([(23, 4), 42, 'a string'])
```

```
>>> mind = set([42, 'a string', 40, 41])
>>> mind
set([40, 41, 42, 'a string'])
>>> mind = set([42, 'a string', 40, 0])
>>> mind
set([40, 0, 42, 'a string'])
>>> mind.add('hello')
>>> mind
set([40, 0, 42, 'a string', 'hello'])
```

Note that sets are unordered, items you add into sets will end up in an indeterminable position, and it may also change from time to time.

```
>>> mind.add('duplicate value')
>>> mind.add('duplicate value')
>>> mind
set([0, 'a string', 40, 42, 'hello', 'duplicate value'])
```

Sets cannot contain a single value more than once. Unlike lists, which can contain anything, the types of data that can be included in sets is restricted. A set can only contain hashable, immutable data types. Integers, strings, and tuples are hashable; lists, dictionaries, and other sets (except frozensets, see below) are not.

Frozenset

The relationship between frozenset and set is like the relationship between tuple and list. Frozenset is an immutable version of set. An example:

```
>>> frozen=frozenset(['life','universe','everything'])
>>> frozen
frozenset({'universe', 'life', 'everything'})
```

Other data types

Python also has other types of arrays, although these are less frequently used and they need to be imported from the standard library before used. We will only brush on them here.

array

> A typed-list, an array may only contain homogeneous values.

collections.defaultdict

> A dictionary that, when an element is not found, returns a default value instead of error.

collections.deque

> A double ended queue, allows fast manipulation on both sides of the queue.

heapq

> A priority queue.

Queue

> A thread-safe multi-producer, multi-consumer queue for use with multi-threaded programs. Note that a list can also be used as queue in a single-threaded code.

For further explanation on set, see *Data Structure/Sets*

3rd party data structure

Some useful data types in Python don't come in the standard library. Some of these are very specialized on their use. We'll mention some of the more well known 3rd party types.

numpy.array

> useful for heavy number crunching

sorteddict

> like the name says, a sorted dictionary

more

> this list isn't comprehensive

Notes

Previous: Basic Math	Index	Next: Source Documentation and Comments

Python Programming/Source Documentation and Comments

Previous: Sequences	Index	Next: Modules and how to use them

Documentation is the process of leaving information about your code. The two mechanisms for doing this in Python are comments and documentation strings.

Comments

There will always be a time in which you have to return to your code. Perhaps it is to fix a bug, or to add a new feature. Regardless, looking at your own code after six months is almost as bad as looking at someone else's code. What one needs is a means to leave reminders to yourself as to what you were doing.

For this purpose, you leave comments. Comments are little snippets of text embedded inside your code that are ignored by the Python interpreter. A comment is denoted by the hash character (#) and extends to the end of the line. For example:

```
#!/usr/bin/env python
# commentexample.py

# Display the knights that come after Scene 24
print("The Knights Who Say Ni!")
# print("I will never see the light of day!")
```

As you can see, you can also use comments to temporarily remove segments of your code, like the second print statement.

Comment Guidelines

The following guidelines are from PEP 8 [1], written by Guido van Rossum.

- General

  - Comments that contradict the code are worse than no comments. Always make a priority of keeping the comments up-to-date when the code changes!
  - Comments should be complete sentences. If a comment is a phrase or sentence, its first word should be capitalized, unless it is an identifier that begins with a lower case letter (never alter the case of identifiers!).
  - If a comment is short, the period at the end can be omitted. Block comments generally consist of one or more paragraphs built out of complete sentences, and each sentence should end in a period.
  - You should use two spaces after a sentence-ending period.
  - When writing English, Strunk and White applies.
  - Python coders from non-English speaking countries: please write your comments in English, unless you are 120% sure that the code will never be read by people who don't speak your language.

- Inline Comments

  - An inline comment is a comment on the same line as a statement. Inline comments should be separated by at least two spaces from the statement. They should start with a # and a single space.
  - Inline comments are unnecessary and in fact distracting if they state the obvious. Don't do this:

```python
x = x + 1 # Increment x
```

But sometimes, this is useful:

```python
x = x + 1 # Compensate for border
```

Documentation Strings

But what if you just want to know how to use a function, class, or method? You could add comments before the function, but comments are inside the code, so you would have to pull up a text editor and view them that way. But you can't pull up comments from a C extension, so that is less than ideal. You could always write a separate text file with how to call the functions, but that would mean that you would have to remember to update that file. If only there was a mechanism for being able to embed the documentation and get at it easily...

Fortunately, Python has such a capability. Documentation strings (or docstrings) are used to create easily-accessible documentation. You can add a docstring to a function, class, or module by adding a string as the first indented statement. For example:

```python
#!/usr/bin/env python
# docstringexample.py


"""Example of using documentation strings."""


class Knight:
    """

    An example class.

    Call spam to get bacon.
    """


    def spam(eggs="bacon"):
        """Prints the argument given."""
```

```
    print(eggs)
```

The convention is to use triple-quoted strings, because it makes it easier to add more documentation spanning multiple lines.

To access the documentation, you can use the help function inside a Python shell with the object you want help on, or you can use the pydoc command from your system's shell. If we were in the directory where docstringexample.py lives, one could enter pydoc docstringexample to get documentation on that module.

Previous: Sequences	Index	Next: Modules and how to use them

References

[1] http://www.python.org/dev/peps/pep-0008/

Python Programming/Modules and how to use them

Previous: Source Documentation and Comments	Index	Next: Files

Modules are libraries that can be called from other scripts. For example, a popular module is the time module. You can call it using:

```
import time
```

Then, create a new python file, you can name it anything (except time.py, since it'd mess up python's module importing, you'll see why later):

```
import time

def main():
    #define the variable 'current_time' as a tuple of time.localtime()
    current_time = time.localtime()
    print(current_time) # print the tuple
    # if the year is 2009 (first value in the current_time tuple)
    if current_time[0] == 2009:
        print('The year is 2009') # print the year

if __name__ == '__main__': # if the function is the main function ...
    main() # ...call it
```

Modules can be called in a various number of ways. For example, we could import the time module as t:

```
import time as t # import the time module and call it 't'

def main():
    current_time = t.localtime()
    print(current_time)
    if current_time[0] == 2009:
        print('The year is 2009')
```

```
if __name__ == '__main__':
    main()
```

It is not necessary to import the whole module, if you only need a certain function or class. To do this, you can do a from-import. Note that a from-import would import the name directly into the global namespace, so when invoking the imported function, it is unnecessary (and wrong) to call the module again:

```
from time import localtime #1

def main():
    current_time = localtime() #2
    print(current_time)
    if current_time[0] == 2009:
        print 'The year is 2009'

if __name__ == '__main__':
    main()
```

it is possible to alias a name imported through from-import

```
from time import localtime as lt

def main():
    current_time = lt()
    print(current_time)
    if current_time[0] == 2009:
        print('The year is 2009')

if __name__ == '__main__':
    main()
```

Previous: Source Documentation and Comments	Index	Next: Files

Python Programming/Files

Previous: Modules and how to use them	Index	Next: Text

File I/O

Read entire file:

```
inputFileText = open("testit.txt", "r").read()
print(inputFileText)
```

In this case the "r" parameter means the file will be opened in read-only mode.

Read certain amount of bytes from a file:

```
inputFileText = open("testit.txt", "r").read(123)
print(inputFileText)
```

When opening a file, one starts reading at the beginning of the file, if one would want more random access to the file, it is possible to use seek() to change the current position in a file and tell() to get to know the current position in the file. This is illustrated in the following example:

```
>>> f=open("/proc/cpuinfo","r")
>>> f.tell()
0L
>>> f.read(10)
'processor\t'
>>> f.read(10)
': 0\nvendor'
>>> f.tell()
20L
>>> f.seek(10)
>>> f.tell()
10L
>>> f.read(10)
': 0\nvendor'
>>> f.close()
>>> f
<closed file '/proc/cpuinfo', mode 'r' at 0xb7d79770>
```

Here a file is opened, twice ten bytes are read, tell() shows that the current offset is at position 20, now seek() is used to go back to position 10 (the same position where the second read was started) and ten bytes are read and printed again. And when no more operations on a file are needed the close() function is used to close the file we opened.

Read one line at a time:

```
for line in open("testit.txt", "r"):
    print line
```

In this case readlines() will return an array containing the individual lines of the file as array entries. Reading a single line can be done using the readline() function which returns the current line as a string. This example will output an additional newline between the individual lines of the file, this is because one is read from the file and print introduces another newline.

Write to a file requires the second parameter of open() to be "w", this will overwrite the existing contents of the file if it already exists when opening the file:

```
outputFileText = "Here's some text to save in a file"
open("testit.txt", "w").write(outputFileText)
```

Append to a file requires the second parameter of open() to be "a" (from append):

```
outputFileText = "Here's some text to add to the existing file."
open("testit.txt", "a").write(outputFileText)
```

Note that this does not add a line break between the existing file content and the string to be added.

Testing Files

Determine whether path exists:

```
import os
os.path.exists('<path string>')
```

When working on systems such as Microsoft Windows(tm), the directory separators will conflict with the path string. To get around this, do the following:

```
import os
os.path.exists('C:\\windows\\example\\path')
```

A better way however is to use "raw", or r:

```
import os
os.path.exists(r'C:\windows\example\path')
```

But there are some other convenient functions in os.path, where path.code.exists() only confirms whether or not path exists, there are functions which let you know if the path is a file, a directory, a mount point or a symlink. There is even a function os.path.realpath() which reveals the true destination of a symlink:

```
>>> import os
>>> os.path.isfile("/")
False
>>> os.path.isfile("/proc/cpuinfo")
True
>>> os.path.isdir("/")
True
>>> os.path.isdir("/proc/cpuinfo")
False
>>> os.path.ismount("/")
True
>>> os.path.islink("/")
False
>>> os.path.islink("/vmlinuz")
True
>>> os.path.realpath("/vmlinuz")
'/boot/vmlinuz-2.6.24-21-generic'
```

Common File Operations

To copy or move a file, use the shutil library.

```
import shutil
shutil.move("originallocation.txt","newlocation.txt")
shutil.copy("original.txt","copy.txt")
```

To perform a recursive copy it is possible to use copytree(), to perform a recursive remove it is possible to use rmtree()

```
import shutil
shutil.copytree("dir1","dir2")
shutil.rmtree("dir1")
```

To remove an individual file there exists the remove() function in the os module:

```
import os
os.remove("file.txt")
```

Previous: Modules and how to use them	Index	Next: Text

Python Programming/Text

Previous: Files	Index	Next: Errors

Get the length of a string:

```
len("Hello Wikibooks!") -> 16
```

Get ASCII character code, or get a character version of it:

```
ord('h') -> 104
chr(65) -> 'A'
```

Previous: Files	Index	Next: Errors

Python Programming/Errors

Previous:	Index	Next:
Text		Namespace

In python there are two types of errors; *syntax errors* and *exceptions*.

Syntax errors

Syntax errors are the most basic type of error. They arise when the Python parser is unable to understand a line of code. Syntax errors are always fatal, i.e. there is no way to successfully execute a piece of code containing syntax errors.

Exceptions

Exceptions arise when the python parser knows what to do with a piece of code but is unable to perform the action. An example would be trying to access the internet with python without an internet connection; the python interpreter knows what to do with that command but is unable to perform it.

Dealing with exceptions

Unlike syntax errors, exceptions are not always fatal. Exceptions can be handled with the use of a `try` statement.

Consider the following code to display the HTML of the website 'goat.com'. When the execution of the program reaches the try statement it will attempt to perform the indented code following, if for some reason there is an error (the computer is not connected to the internet or something) the python interpreter will jump to the indented code below the 'except:' command.

```python
import urllib2
url = 'http://www.goat.com'
try:
    req = urllib2.Request(url)
    response = urllib2.urlopen(req)
    the_page = response.read()
    print the_page
except:
    print "We have a problem."
```

Another way to handle an error is to except a specific error.

```python
try:
    age = int(raw_input("Enter your age: "))
    print "You must be {0} years old.".format(age)
except ValueError:
    print "Your age must be numeric."
```

If the user enters a numeric value as his/her age, the output should look like this:

```
Enter your age: 5
You must be 5 years old.
```

However, if the user enters a non-numeric value as his/her age, a `ValueError` is thrown when trying to execute the `int()` method on a non-numeric string, and the code under the `except` clause is executed:

```
Enter your age: five
Your age must be a number.
```

You can also use a `try` block with a `while` loop to validate input:

```
valid = False
while valid == False:
    try:
        age = int(raw_input("Enter your age: "))
        valid = True      # This statement will only execute if the
above statement executes without error.
        print "You must be {0} years old.".format(age)
    except ValueError:
        print "Your age must be numeric."
```

The program will prompt you for your age until you enter a valid age:

```
Enter your age: five
Your age must be numeric.
Enter your age: abc10
Your age must be numeric.
Enter your age: 15
You must be 15 years old.
```

Previous: Text	Index	Next: Namespace

Python Programming/Namespace

Previous: Errors	Index	Next: Object-oriented programming

Previous: Errors	Index	Next: Object-oriented programming

Python Programming/Object-oriented programming

Previous: Namespace	Index	Next: User Interaction

Object Oriented Programming

OOP is a programming approach where objects are defined with methods (functions, actions or events) and properties (values, characteristics), resulting in more readable, more reusable code.

Lets say you're writing a program where you need to keep track of multiple cars. Each car has different characteristics like mileage, color, and top speed, but lucky for us they all can perform some common actions like braking, accelerating, and turning.

Instead of writing code separately for each car we could create a class called 'Car' that will be the blueprint for each particular car.

Constructing a Class

Class is the name given to a generic description of an object. In python you define a class method (an action, event, or function) using the following structure:

```
class <<name>>:
    def <<method>> (self [, <<optional arguments>>]):
        <<Function codes>>
```

Let's take a detailed look. We define our object using the 'class' keyword, the name we want, and a colon. We define its methods as we would a normal function: only one indent with 'self' as its first argument (we get to this later). So our example car class may look like this:

```
class Car:
    def brake(self):
        print("Brakes")

    def accelerate(self):
        print("Accelerating")
```

But how do I use it?

Once you have created the class, you actually need to create an object for each instance of that class. In python we create a new variable to create an instance of a class. Example:

```
car1 = Car() # car 1 is my instance for the first car
car2 = Car()

# And use the object methods like
car1.brake()
```

Using the parentheses ("calling" the class) tells Python that you want to create an instance and not just copy the class definition. You would need to create a variable for each car. However, now each car object can take advantage of the class methods and attributes, so you don't need to write a brake and accelerate function for each car independently.

Properties

Right now all the cars look the same, but let's give them some properties to differentiate them. A property is just a variable that is specific to a given object. To assign a property we write it like:

```
car1.color = "Red"
```

And retrieve its value like:

```
print(car1.color)
```

It is good programming practice to write functions to *get* (or retrieve) and *set* (or assign) properties that are not 'read-only'. For example:

```
class Car:
    ... previous methods ...

    def set_owner(self,Owners_Name): # This will set the owner property
        self._owner = Owners_Name

    def get_owner(self): # This will retrieve the owner property
        return self._owner
```

Notice the single underscore before the property name; this is a way of hiding variable names from users.

Beginning from Python 2.2, you may also define the above example in a way that looks like a normal variable:

```
class Car:
    ... previous methods ...
    owner = property(get_owner, set_owner)
```

When code such as `mycar.owner = "John Smith"` is used, the set_owner function is called transparently.

Extending a Class

Let's say we want to add more functions to our class, but we are reluctant to change its code for fear that this might mess up programs that depend on its current version. The solution is to 'extend' our class. When you extend a class you inherit all the parent methods and properties and can add new ones. For example, we can add a start_car method to our car class. To extend a class we supply the name of the parent class in parentheses after the new class name, for example:

```python
class New_car(Car):
    def start_car(self):
        self.on = true
```

This new class extends the parent class.

Special Class Methods

A Constructor is a method that gets called whenever you create a new instance of a class. In python you create a constructor by writing a function inside the method name __init__. It can even accept arguments, e.g. to set attribute values upon creating a new instance of the class. For instance, we could create a new car object and set its brand, model, and year attributes on a single line, rather than expending an additional line for each attribute:

```python
class New_car(Car):
    def __init__(self,brand, model, year):
        # Sets all the properties
        self.brand = brand
        self.model = model
        self.year = year

    def start_car(self):
        """ Start the cars engine """
        print ("vroem vroem")

if __name__ == "__main__":
    # Creates two instances of new_car, each with unique properties
    car1 = New_car("Ford","F-150",2001)
    car2 = New_car("Toyota","Corolla",2007)

    car1.start_car()
    car2.start_car()
```

For more information on classes go to the Class Section in this book.

Previous: Namespace	Index	Next: User Interaction

Python Programming/User Interaction

| Previous: Object-oriented programming | Index | Next: Databases |

Scripts don't normally take user input since they are usually designed to perform small useful tasks. However, there are times where user input is really important. There are two ways to retrieve user input: the first is using the console window (Command Line Interface) and the second is using the Graphical User Interface (GUI).

Console Windows (Command Line Interface)

Python has two built in functions to retrieve users input on a console; the first is **input()** and the second one is **raw_input()**. These two functions have different purposes and both accept a string argument which is displayed on the terminal before accepting the user input.

The **input()** function expects a python instruction as the user input. This means that the user response must be python coded - strings must include quotes or double quotes. Once this function is called, the input entered by the user will be evaluated, and return the result to the application. This can make it a security risk in some cases, unless you're planning to be the only user of the application.

While the **raw_input()** function expects any type of input and returns a python string, this second function fits more of our current needs.

```python
# Ask user for his name and stores
name = raw_input("Please enter your name:")
# Display the name entered by the user.
print name
```

If the information entered by the user needs to be numeric to perform some calculation the return value most be converted using the **float()** or **int()** conversion function.

```python
# Retrieve user age
age = int(raw_input("Please enter your age:"))
print age
```

As you may expect coding all the input for a big application and all the validation will increase the file size. To make steps simpler we can create an object (using a Class) that handles retrieving the data and validating.

```python
class ainput:     # We can't use input as it is a existent function name,
 so we use AInput for Advance Input
    ''' This class will create a object with a simpler coding interface
to retrieve console input'''
    def __init__(self,msg=""):
        ''' This will create a instance of ainput object'''
        self.data = ""    # Initialize a empty data variable
        if not msg == "":
            self.ask(msg)

    def ask(self,msg, req=0):
        ''' This will display the prompt and retrieve the user input.'''
        if req == 0:
```

```
        self.data = raw_input(msg)    # Save the user input to a local
object variable
        else:
            self.data = raw_input(msg + " (Require)")

        # Verify that the information was entered and its not empty. This
will accept a space character. Better Validation needed
        if req == 1 and self.data == "":
            self.ask(msg,req)

    def getString(self):
        ''' Returns the user input as String'''
        return self.data


    def getInteger(self):
        ''' Returns the user input as a Integer'''
        return int(self.data)


    def getNumber(self):
        ''' Returns the user input as a Float number'''
        return float(self.data)
```

With this tool at our disposal displaying, retrieving and validating user input is a breeze. The use of the code will run like this. For this example we are using a single line to display the call and retrieve the information.

```
# import is not imported
name = ainput("Please enter your first name:").getString()
age = ainput("Now enter your age:").getInteger()
print name, age
```

To test this code copy the following to a python script file (e.g. userInteraction.py)

```
class ainput:    # We can't use input as it is a existent function name,
 so we use AInput for Advance Input
    ''' This class will create a object with a simpler coding interface
to retrieve console input'''
    def __init__(self,msg=""):
        ''' This will create a instance of ainput object'''
        self.data = ""   # Initialize a empty data variable
        if not msg == "":
            self.ask(msg)


    def ask(self,msg, req=0):
        ''' This will display the prompt and retrieve the user input.'''
        if req == 0:
            self.data = raw_input(msg)    # Save the user input to a local
object variable
        else:
            self.data = raw_input(msg + " (Require)")
```

```
      # Verify that the information was entered and its not empty. This
will accept a space character. Better Validation needed
      if req == 1 and self.data == "":
          self.ask(msg,req)

  def getString(self):
      ''' Returns the user input as String'''
      return self.data

  def getInteger(self):
      ''' Returns the user input as a Integer'''
      return int(self.data)

  def getNumber(self):
      ''' Returns the user input as a Float number'''
      return float(self.data)

def main():
      # import is not imported
      name = ainput("Please enter your first name:").getString()
      age = ainput("Now enter your age:").getInteger()
      print name, age

if __name__ == '__main__':
      main()
```

Graphical User Interface(GUI)

Python has many different GUI toolkits, of which the most standard is Tkinter which comes with Python. This section will be limited to basic Tkinter programming fundamentals, a more detailed reference can be found in GUI Programming Modules of this wikibook.

Lets proceed by creating a classic developer Hello World example with the following code.

```
import Tkinter

# Define input retrieve function for application input
def retrieve_text():
  print app_entry.get()

if __name__ == "__main__":

  # Create Window Object or Window Form
  app_win = Tkinter.Tk()

  # Create label object
  app_label = Tkinter.Label(app_win,text="Hello World")
  app_label.pack()
```

```
    # Create User Input Object
    app_entry = Tkinter.Entry(app_win)
    app_entry.pack()

    # Create Button Object
    app_button = Tkinter.Button(app_win,text="Print
Value",command=retrieve_text)
    app_button.pack()

    # Initialize Graphical Loop
    app_win.mainloop()
```

On the first line we actually import the Tkinter library in use by using import Tkinter. Next a function is created to retrieve the value from the input object use in the GUI. For the moment the value will be print to the console.

Next we create a windows object where all the gui components (or widgets as the Tkinter toolkit calls them) are place. Think of it like a painting canvas where we draw our application interface.

Having define the windows we proceed to create a Label widget. Notice the first argument on Label object call is the variable holding the window object this is for binding purpose, the next argument is the label text. The next line binds the Label object to the Window object by using the pack method.

Next stop is the User Input Object, the Tkinter library provides the Entry Object (same as Textbox in other programming languages). Notice that again we need the Window object as first argument. The next lines bind the entry object with the window.

Next is the creation of the Button Object for the application. Like all the other Objects the Window object its the first argument. The Button Text value is fill much like the same as we did with the label and the buttons action is fill using the command argument. *Notice that the command argument doesn't have quote as its not a string text but a reference to the function.* The next line proceeds to bind the Button to the window.

On the last line a call to app_win.mainloop() allow the Tkinter application to run.

Advance OOP GUI

So far it seems tedious to create a GUI using Python, especially with so much code to write for such a simple program. But when you bring OOP concepts into the mix it is different. For a moment think of an application that requires a couple of inputs with labels to identify them. The OOP methodolgy has the advantage of letting us create a new object that presents the label and entry object at the same time, is reusable and can be called with one line of code.

The code below does just that, it wraps a label and a entry object inside a Tkinter Frame Object. The object require windows object as first argument and the label text as the second, while the **text** function returns a string value for the user input. A more advanced text box can include validation and data retrieval.

```
# Import Tkinter Library
import Tkinter

# Define our Textbox Object
class textbox(Tkinter.Frame):

    # Object Initialize
    def __init__(self,parent, msg):
```

```
        # Initialize the Frame properties by explicit calling its Init
method
        Tkinter.Frame.__init__(self,parent)

        # Create the Textbox Label on the Left side
        self.g_label = Tkinter.Label(self,text=msg)
        self.g_label.pack(side=Tkinter.LEFT,expand=False)

        # Create the Textbox Entry on the Right side
        self.g_entry = Tkinter.Entry(self)
        self.g_entry.pack(side=Tkinter.LEFT, fill=Tkinter.X,
expand=True)

        # Proceed to pack the frame
        self.pack(fill=Tkinter.X, anchor=Tkinter.NW, expand=True)


    def text(self):
        # Textbox text value retrieval
        return self.gui['entry'].get()
```

Now on our multi-input application we can use this new object with one simple line for each instance:

```
name = textbox(win,"Name:")
```

Notice that we don't need to call the pack method as the text box object packs itself on the last line of the __init__. This is not practical on complex layout application since the object controls this function, but works wonders for small script GUI.

Previous: Object-oriented programming	Index	Next: Databases

Python Programming/Databases

Previous: User Interaction	Index	Next: Internet

Python has some support for working with databases. Modules included with Python include modules for SQLite and Berkeley DB. Modules for MySQL and PostgreSQL and others are available as third-party modules. The latter have to be downloaded and installed before use.

MySQL

An Example with MySQL would look like this:

```
1  import MySQLdb
2  db = MySQLdb.connect("host machine", "dbuser", "password", "dbname")
3  cursor = db.cursor()
4  query = """SELECT * FROM sampletable"""
5  lines = cursor.execute(query)
6  data = cursor.fetchall()
7  db.close()
```

On the first line, the Module MySQLdb is imported. Then a connection to the database is set up and on line 4, we save the actual SQL statement to be executed in the variable query. On line 5 we execute the query and on line 6 we fetch all the data. After the execution of this piece of code, lines contains the number of lines fetched (e.g. the number of rows in the table sampletable). The variable data contains all the actual data, e.g. the content of sampletable. In the end, the connection to the database would be closed again. If the number of lines are large, it is better to use row = cursor.fetchone() and process the rows individually:

```
#first 5 lines are the same as above
while True:
  row = cursor.fetchone()
  if row == None: break
  #do something with this row of data
db.close()
```

Obviously, some kind of data processing has to be used on row, otherwise the data will not be stored. The result of the fetchone() command is a Tuple.

In order to make the initialization of the connection easier, a configuration file can be used:

```
import MySQLdb
db = MySQLdb.connect(read_default_file="~/.my.cnf")
...
```

Here, the file .my.cnf in the home directory contains the necessary configuration information for MySQL.

External links

- SQLite documentation [1]
- Psycopg2 (PostgreSQL module - newer) [2]
- PyGreSQL (PostgreSQL module - older) [3]
- MySQL module [4]

Previous: User Interaction	Index	Next: Internet

References

[1] http://docs.python.org/library/sqlite3.html

[2] http://initd.org/

[3] http://www.pygresql.org/

[4] http://sourceforge.net/projects/mysql-python/

Python Programming/Internet

Previous: Databases	Index	Next: Networks

The urllib module which is bundled with python can be used for web interaction. This module provides a file-like interface for web urls.

Getting page text as a string

An example of reading the contents of a webpage

```python
import urllib
pageText = urllib.urlopen("http://www.spam.org/eggs.html").read()
print pageText
```

Get and post methods can be used, too.

```python
import urllib
params = urllib.urlencode({"plato":1, "socrates":10, "sophokles":4,
"arkhimedes":11})

# Using GET method
pageText =
urllib.urlopen("http://international-philosophy.com/greece?%s" %
params).read()
print pageText

# Using POST method
pageText = urllib.urlopen("http://international-philosophy.com/greece",
 params).read()
print pageText
```

Downloading files

To save the content of a page on the internet directly to a file, you can read() it and save it as a string to a file object, or you can use the urlretrieve function:

```
import urllib
urllib.urlretrieve("http://upload.wikimedia.org/wikibooks/en/9/91/Python_Programming.pdf",
 "pythonbook.pdf")
```

This will download the file from here [1] and save it to a file "pythonbook.pdf" on your hard drive.

Other functions

The urllib module includes other functions that may be helpful when writing programs that use the internet:

```
>>> plain_text = "This isn't suitable for putting in a URL"
>>> print urllib.quote(plain_text)
This%20isn%27t%20suitable%20for%20putting%20in%20a%20URL
>>> print urllib.quote_plus(plain_text)
This+isn%27t+suitable+for+putting+in+a+URL
```

The urlencode function, described above converts a dictionary of key-value pairs into a query string to pass to a URL, the quote and quote_plus functions encode normal strings. The quote_plus function uses plus signs for spaces, for use in submitting data for form fields. The unquote and unquote_plus functions do the reverse, converting urlencoded text to plain text.

| Previous: Databases | Index | Next: Networks |

References

[1] http://upload.wikimedia.org/wikibooks/en/9/91/Python_Programming.pdf

Python Programming/Networks

| Previous: Internet | Index | Next: Tips and Tricks |

| Previous: Internet | Index | Next: Tips and Tricks |

Python Programming/Tips and Tricks

| Previous: Networks | Index | Next: Basic syntax |

There are many tips and tricks you can learn in Python:

Strings

- Triple quotes are an easy way to define a string with both single and double quotes.
- String concatenation is *expensive*. Use percent formatting and str.join() for concatenation:

(but don't worry about this unless your resulting string is more then 500-1000 characters long) [1]

```
print "Spam" + " eggs" + " and" + " spam"          # DON'T DO THIS
print " ".join(["Spam","eggs","and","spam"])       # Much
faster/more
                                                   # common Python
 idiom
print "%s %s %s %s" % ("Spam", "eggs", "and", "spam")   # Also a
pythonic way of
                                                   # doing it -
very fast
```

Module choice

- cPickle is a faster, C written module for pickle. cPickle is used to serialize python program. Other modules have C implementations as well, cStringIO for the StringIO module, and cProfile for the profile module.

```
import cPickle # You may want to import it as P for convenience.
```

List comprehension and generators

- List comprehension and generator expressions are very useful for working with small, compact loops. Additionally, it is faster than a normal for-loop.

```
directory = os.listdir(os.getcwd())        # Gets a list of files in the
                                           # directory the program runs
from
filesInDir = [item for item in directory] # Normal For Loop rules
apply, you
```

```
                                                      # can add "if condition" to
make a
                                                      # more narrow search.
```

- List comprehension and generator expression can be used to work with two (or more) lists with zip or itertools.izip

```
[a - b for (a,b) in zip((1,2,3), (1,2,3))]  # will return [0, 0, 0]
```

Data type choice

Choosing the correct data type can be critical to the performance of an application. For example, say you have 2 lists:

```
list1 = [{'a': 1, 'b': 2}, {'c': 3, 'd': 4}, {'e': 5, 'f': 6}]
list2 = [{'e': 5, 'f': 6}, {'g': 7, 'h': 8}, {'i': 9, 'j': 10}]
```

and you want to find the entries common to both lists. You could iterate over one list, checking for common items in the other:

```
common = []
for entry in list1:
    if entry in list2:
        common.append(entry)
```

For such small lists, this will work fine, but for larger lists, for example if each contains thousands of entries, the following will be more efficient, and produces the same result:

```
set1 = set([tuple(entry.items()) for entry in list1])
set2 = set([tuple(entry.items()) for entry in list2])
common = set1.intersection(set2)
common = [dict(entry) for entry in common]
```

Sets are optimized for speed in such functions. Dictionaries themselves cannot be used as members of a set as they are mutable, but tuples can. If one needs to do set operations on a list of dictionaries, one can convert the items to tuples and the list to a set, perform the operation, then convert back. This is often much faster than trying to replicate set operations using string functions.

Other

- Decorators can be used for handling common concerns like logging, db access, etc.
- While Python has no built-in function to flatten a list you can use a recursive function to do the job quickly.

```
def flatten(seq, a = None):
    """flatten(seq, a = None) -> list

    Return a flat version of the iterator `seq` appended to `a`
    """
    if a == None:
        a = []
    try:                                # Can `seq` be iterated over?
        for item in seq:                # If so then iterate over `seq`
            flatten(item, a)            # and make the same check on each
```

```
item.
    except TypeError:          # If seq isn't iterable
        a.append(seq)          # append it to the new list.
    return a
```

- To stop a Python script from closing right after you launch one independently, add this code:

```
print 'Hit Enter to exit'
raw_input()
```

- Python already has a GUI interface built in: Tkinter

Not complete. Add more, please [2].

References

[1] "'concat vs join - followup' on 'Python Rocks! and other rants 27.8.2004 Weblog of Kent S Johnson'" (http://www.pycs.net/users/ 0000323/weblog/2004/08/27.html). August 27, 2004. . Retrieved 2008-08-29.

[2] http://en.wikibooks.org/w/index.php?title=Python_Programming/Tips_and_Tricks&action=edit

Previous: Networks	Index	Next: Basic syntax

Concepts

Python Programming/Basic syntax

Previous: Tips and Tricks	Index	Next: Data types

There are five fundamental concepts in Python.

Case Sensitivity

All variables are case-sensitive. Python treats 'number' and 'Number' as separate, unrelated entities.

Spaces and tabs don't mix

Because whitespace is significant, remember that spaces and tabs don't mix, so use only one or the other when indenting your programs. A common error is to mix them. While they may look the same in editor, the interpreter will read them differently and it will result in either an error or unexpected behavior. Most decent text editors can be configured to let tab key emit spaces instead.

Python's Style Guideline described that the preferred way is using 4 spaces.

⭐ Tips: If you invoked python from the command-line, you can give -t or -tt argument to python to make python issue a warning or error on inconsistent tab usage.

```
pythonprogrammer@wikibook:~$ python -tt myscript.py
```

this will issue an error if you mixed spaces and tabs.

Objects

In Python, like all object oriented languages, there are aggregations of code and data called Objects, which typically represent the pieces in a conceptual model of a system.

Objects in Python are created (i.e., instantiated) from templates called Classes (which are covered later, as much of the language can be used without understanding classes). They have "attributes", which represent the various pieces of code and data which comprise the object. To access attributes, one writes the name of the object followed by a period (henceforth called a dot), followed by the name of the attribute.

An example is the 'upper' attribute of strings, which refers to the code that returns a copy of the string in which all the letters are uppercase. To get to this, it is necessary to have a way to refer to the object (in the following example, the way is the literal string that constructs the object).

```
'bob'.upper
```

Code attributes are called "methods". So in this example, upper is a method of 'bob' (as it is of all strings). To execute the code in a method, use a matched pair of parentheses surrounding a comma separated list of whatever arguments the method accepts (upper doesn't accept any arguments). So to find an uppercase version of the string 'bob', one could use the following:

```
'bob'.upper()
```

Scope

In a large system, it is important that one piece of code does not affect another in difficult to predict ways. One of the simplest ways to further this goal is to prevent one programmer's choice of names from preventing another from choosing that name. Because of this, the concept of scope was invented. A scope is a "region" of code in which a name can be used and outside of which the name cannot be easily accessed. There are two ways of delimiting regions in Python: with functions or with modules. They each have different ways of accessing the useful data that was produced within the scope from outside the scope. With functions, that way is to return the data. The way to access names from other modules lead us to another concept.

Namespaces

It would be possible to teach Python without the concept of namespaces because they are so similar to attributes, which we have already mentioned, but the concept of namespaces is one that transcends any particular programming language, and so it is important to teach. To begin with, there is a built-in function **dir()** that can be used to help one understand the concept of namespaces. When you first start the Python interpreter (i.e., in interactive mode), you can list the objects in the current (or default) namespace using this function.

```
Python 2.3.4 (#53, Oct 18 2004, 20:35:07) [MSC v.1200 32 bit (Intel)]
on win32
Type "help", "copyright", "credits" or "license" for more information.
>>> dir()
['__builtins__', '__doc__', '__name__']
```

This function can also be used to show the names available within a module namespace. To demonstrate this, first we can use the **type()** function to show what __builtins__ is:

```
>>> type(__builtins__)
<type 'module'>
```

Since it is a module, we can list the names within the __builtins__ namespace, again using the **dir()** function (note the complete list of names has been abbreviated):

```
>>> dir(__builtins__)
['ArithmeticError', ... 'copyright', 'credits', ... 'help', ...
'license', ... 'zip']
>>>
```

Namespaces are a simple concept. A namespace is a place in which a name resides. Each name within a namespace is distinct from names outside of the namespace. This layering of namespaces is called scope. A name is placed within a namespace when that name is given a value. For example:

```
>>> dir()
['__builtins__', '__doc__', '__name__']
>>> name = "Bob"
>>> import math
>>> dir()
['__builtins__', '__doc__', '__name__', 'math', 'name']
```

Note that I was able to add the "name" variable to the namespace using a simple assignment statement. The import statement was used to add the "math" name to the current namespace. To see what math is, we can simply:

```
>>> math
<module 'math' (built-in)>
```

Since it is a module, it also has a namespace. To display the names within this namespace, we:

```
>>> dir(math)
['__doc__', '__name__', 'acos', 'asin', 'atan', 'atan2', 'ceil', 'cos',
 'cosh', 'degrees', 'e',
'exp', 'fabs', 'floor', 'fmod', 'frexp', 'hypot', 'ldexp', 'log',
'log10', 'modf', 'pi', 'pow',
'radians', 'sin', 'sinh', 'sqrt', 'tan', 'tanh']
>>>
```

If you look closely, you will notice that both the default namespace, and the math module namespace have a '__name__' object. The fact that each layer can contain an object with the same name is what scope is all about. To access objects inside a namespace, simply use the name of the module, followed by a dot, followed by the name of the object. This allow us to differentiate between the __name__ object within the current namespace, and that of the object with the same name within the math module. For example:

```
>>> print __name__
__main__
>>> print math.__name__
math
>>> print math.__doc__
This module is always available.  It provides access to the
mathematical functions defined by the C standard.
>>> math.pi
3.1415926535897931
```

Previous: Tips and Tricks	Index	Next: Data types

Python Programming/Data types

Previous: Basic syntax	Index	Next: Numbers

Data types determine whether an object can do something, or whether it just would not make sense. Other programming languages often determine whether an operation makes sense for an object by making sure the object can never be stored somewhere where the operation will be performed on the object (this type system is called static typing). Python does not do that. Instead it stores the type of an object with the object, and checks when the operation is performed whether that operation makes sense for that object (this is called dynamic typing).

Python's basic datatypes are:

- Integers, equivalent to C longs
- Floating-Point numbers, equivalent to C doubles
- Long integers of non-limited length
- Complex Numbers.
- Strings
- Some others, such as type and function

Python's composite datatypes are:

- lists
- tuples
- dictionaries, also called dicts, hashmaps, or associative arrays

Literal integers can be entered as in C:

- decimal numbers can be entered directly
- octal numbers can be entered by prepending a 0 (0732 is octal 732, for example)
- hexadecimal numbers can be entered by prepending a 0x (0xff is hex FF, or 255 in decimal)

Floating point numbers can be entered directly.

Long integers are entered either directly (1234567891011121314151617181920 is a long integer) or by appending an L (0L is a long integer). Computations involving short integers that overflow are automatically turned into long integers.

Complex numbers are entered by adding a real number and an imaginary one, which is entered by appending a j (i.e. 10+5j is a complex number. So is 10j). Note that j by itself does not constitute a number. If this is desired, use 1j.

Strings can be either single or triple quoted strings. The difference is in the starting and ending delimiters, and in that single quoted strings cannot span more than one line. Single quoted strings are entered by entering either a single quote (') or a double quote (") followed by its match. So therefore

```
'foo' works, and
"moo" works as well,
    but
'bar" does not work, and
"baz' does not work either.
"quux'' is right out.
```

Triple quoted strings are like single quoted strings, but can span more than one line. Their starting and ending delimiters must also match. They are entered with three consecutive single or double quotes, so

```
'''foo''' works, and
"""moo""" works as well,
    but
'"'bar'"' does not work, and
"""baz''' does not work either.
'"'quux"'" is right out.
```

Tuples are entered in parenthesis, with commas between the entries:

```
(10, 'Mary had a little lamb')
```

Also, the parenthesis can be left out when it's not ambiguous to do so:

```
10, 'whose fleece was as white as snow'
```

Note that one-element tuples can be entered by surrounding the entry with parentheses and adding a comma like so:

```
('this is a stupid tuple',)
```

Lists are similar, but with brackets:

```
['abc', 1,2,3]
```

Dicts are created by surrounding with curly braces a list of key,value pairs separated from each other by a colon and from the other entries with commas:

```
{ 'hello': 'world', 'weight': 'African or European?' }
```

Any of these composite types can contain any other, to any depth:

```
((((((((('bob',),['Mary', 'had', 'a', 'little', 'lamb']), { 'hello' :
'world' } ),),),),),),)
```

Previous: Basic syntax	Index	Next: Numbers

Python Programming/Numbers

Previous: Data types	Index	Next: Strings

Python supports 4 types of Numbers, the int, the long, the float and the complex. You don't have to specify what type of variable you want; Python does that automatically.

- *Int:* This is the basic integer type in python, it is equivalent to the hardware 'c long' for the platform you are using.
- *Long:* This is a integer number that's length is non-limited. In python 2.2 and later, Ints are automatically turned into long ints when they overflow.
- *Float:* This is a binary floating point number. Longs and Ints are automatically converted to floats when a float is used in an expression, and with the true-division // operator.
- *Complex:* This is a complex number consisting of two floats. Complex literals are written as a + bj where a and b are floating-point numbers denoting the real and imaginary parts respectively.

In general, the number types are automatically 'up cast' in this order:

Int → Long → Float → Complex. The farther to the right you go, the higher the precedence.

```
>>> x = 5
>>> type(x)
<type 'int'>
>>> x = 18768765456465897097890986957645
>>> type(x)
<type 'long'>
>>> x = 1.34763
>>> type(x)
<type 'float'>
>>> x = 5 + 2j
>>> type(x)
<type 'complex'>
```

However, some expressions may be confusing since in the current version of python, using the / operator on two integers will return another integer, using floor division. For example, 5/2 will give you 2. You have to specify one of the operands as a float to get true division, e.g. 5/2. or 5./2 (the dot specifies you want to work with float) to have 2.5. This behavior is deprecated and will disappear in a future python release as shown from the from __future__ import.

```
>>> 5/2
2
>>>5/2.
2.5
>>>5./2
2.5
>>> from __future__ import division
>>> 5/2
2.5
>>> 5//2
2
```

Previous: Data types	Index	Next:
		Strings

Python Programming/Strings

Previous: Numbers	Index	Next: Lists

String manipulation

String operations

Equality

Two strings are equal if and only if they have *exactly* the same contents, meaning that they are both the same length and each character has a one-to-one positional correspondence. Many other languages test strings only for identity; that is, they only test whether two strings occupy the same space in memory. This latter operation is possible in Python using the operator is.

Example:

```
>>> a = 'hello'; b = 'hello'  # Assign 'hello' to a and b.
>>> print a == b              # True
True
>>> print a == 'hello'        #
True
>>> print a == "hello"        # (choice of delimiter is unimportant)
True
>>> print a == 'hello '       # (extra space)
False
>>> print a == 'Hello'        # (wrong case)
False
```

Numerical

There are two quasi-numerical operations which can be done on strings -- addition and multiplication. String addition is just another name for concatenation. String multiplication is repetitive addition, or concatenation. So:

```
>>> c = 'a'
>>> c + 'b'
'ab'
>>> c * 5
'aaaaa'
```

Containment

There is a simple operator 'in' that returns True if the first operand is contained in the second. This also works on substrings

```
>>> x = 'hello'
>>> y = 'll'
>>> x in y
False
>>> y in x
True
```

Note that 'print x in y' would have also returned the same value.

Indexing and Slicing

Much like arrays in other languages, the individual characters in a string can be accessed by an integer representing its position in the string. The first character in string s would be s[0] and the nth character would be at s[n-1].

```
>>> s = "Xanadu"
>>> s[1]
'a'
```

Unlike arrays in other languages, Python also indexes the arrays backwards, using negative numbers. The last character has index -1, the second to last character has index -2, and so on.

```
>>> s[-4]
'n'
```

We can also use "slices" to access a substring of s. s[a:b] will give us a string starting with s[a] and ending with s[b-1].

```
>>> s[1:4]
'ana'
```

Neither of these is assignable.

```
>>> print s
>>> s[0] = 'J'
Traceback (most recent call last):
File "<stdin>", line 1, in ?
TypeError: object does not support item assignment
>>> s[1:3] = "up"
Traceback (most recent call last):
File "<stdin>", line 1, in ?
TypeError: object does not support slice assignment
>>> print s
```

Outputs (assuming the errors were suppressed):

```
Xanadu
Xanadu
```

Another feature of slices is that if the beginning or end is left empty, it will default to the first or last index, depending on context:

```
>>> s[2:]
'nadu'
>>> s[:3]
'Xan'
>>> s[:]
'Xanadu'
```

You can also use negative numbers in slices:

```
>>> print s[-2:]
'du'
```

To understand slices, it's easiest not to count the elements themselves. It is a bit like counting not on your fingers, but in the spaces between them. The list is indexed like this:

```
Element:       1     2     3     4
Index:    0     1     2     3     4
         -4    -3    -2    -1
```

So, when we ask for the [1:3] slice, that means we start at index 1, and end at index 3, and take everything in between them. If you are used to indexes in C or Java, this can be a bit disconcerting until you get used to it.

String constants

String constants can be found in the standard string module. Either single or double quotes may be used to delimit string constants.

String methods

There are a number of methods of built-in string functions:

- **capitalize**
- **center**
- **count**
- decode
- encode
- endswith
- **expandtabs**
- **find**
- **index**
- **isalnum**
- **isalpha**
- **isdigit**
- **islower**
- **isspace**
- **istitle**
- **isupper**
- **join**
- **ljust**
- **lower**
- **lstrip**
- **replace**

- **rfind**
- **rindex**
- **rjust**
- **rstrip**
- **split**
- **splitlines**
- startswith
- **strip**
- **swapcase**
- **title**
- translate
- **upper**
- zfill

Only emphasized items will be covered.

is*

isalnum(), isalpha(), isdigit(), islower(), isupper(), isspace(), and istitle() fit into this category.

The length of the string object being compared must be at least 1, or the is* methods will return False. In other words, a string object of len(string) == 0, is considered "empty", or False.

- **isalnum** returns True if the string is entirely composed of alphabetic and/or numeric characters (i.e. no punctuation).
- **isalpha** and **isdigit** work similarly for alphabetic characters or numeric characters only.
- **isspace** returns True if the string is composed entirely of whitespace.
- **islower**, **isupper**, and **istitle** return True if the string is in lowercase, uppercase, or titlecase respectively. Uncased characters are "allowed", such as digits, but there must be at least one cased character in the string object in order to return True. Titlecase means the first cased character of each word is uppercase, and any immediately following cased characters are lowercase. Curiously, 'Y2K'.istitle() returns True. That is because uppercase characters can only follow uncased characters. Likewise, lowercase characters can only follow uppercase or lowercase characters. Hint: whitespace is uncased.

Example:

```
>>> '2YK'.istitle()
False
>>> '2Yk'.istitle()
True
>>> '2Y K'.istitle()
True
```

title, upper, lower, swapcase, capitalize

Returns the string converted to title case, upper case, lower case, inverts case, or capitalizes, respectively.

The **title** method capitalizes the first letter of each word in the string (and makes the rest lower case). Words are identified as substrings of alphabetic characters that are separated by non-alphabetic characters, such as digits, or whitespace. This can lead to some unexpected behavior. For example, the string "x1x" will be converted to "X1X" instead of "X1x".

The **swapcase** method makes all uppercase letters lowercase and vice versa.

The **capitalize** method is like title except that it considers the entire string to be a word. (i.e. it makes the first character upper case and the rest lower case)

Example:

```
>>> s = 'Hello, wOrLD'
>>> s
'Hello, wOrLD'
>>> s.title()
'Hello, World'
>>> s.swapcase()
'hELLO, WoRld'
>>> s.upper()
'HELLO, WORLD'
>>> s.lower()
'hello, world'
>>> s.capitalize()
'Hello, world'
```

count

Returns the number of the specified substrings in the string. i.e.

```
>>> s = 'Hello, world'
>>> s.count('l') # print the number of 'l's in 'Hello, World' (3)
3
```

strip, rstrip, lstrip

Returns a copy of the string with the leading (lstrip) and trailing (rstrip) whitespace removed. strip removes both.

```
>>> s = '\t Hello, world\n\t '
>>> print s
         Hello, world

>>> print s.strip()
Hello, world
>>> print s.lstrip()
Hello, world
         # ends here
>>> print s.rstrip()
         Hello, world
```

Note the leading and trailing tabs and newlines.

Strip methods can also be used to remove other types of characters.

```
import string
s = 'www.wikibooks.org'
print s
print s.strip('w')                # Removes all w's from outside
print s.strip(string.lowercase)   # Removes all lowercase letters from
 outside
print s.strip(string.printable)   # Removes all printable characters
```

Outputs:

```
www.wikibooks.org
.wikibooks.org
.wikibooks.
```

Note that string.lowercase and string.printable require an import string statement

ljust, rjust, center

left, right or center justifies a string into a given field size (the rest is padded with spaces).

```
>>> s = 'foo'
>>> s
'foo'
>>> s.ljust(7)
'foo    '
>>> s.rjust(7)
'    foo'
>>> s.center(7)
'  foo  '
```

join

Joins together the given sequence with the string as separator:

```
>>> seq = ['1', '2', '3', '4', '5']
>>> ' '.join(seq)
'1 2 3 4 5'
>>> '+'.join(seq)
'1+2+3+4+5'
```

map may be helpful here: (it converts numbers in seq into strings)

```
>>> seq = [1,2,3,4,5]
>>> ' '.join(map(str, seq))
'1 2 3 4 5'
```

now arbitrary objects may be in seq instead of just strings.

find, index, rfind, rindex

The find and index methods returns the index of the first found occurrence of the given subsequence. If it is not found, find returns -1 but index raises a ValueError. rfind and rindex are the same as find and index except that they search through the string from right to left (i.e. they find the last occurrence)

```
>>> s = 'Hello, world'
>>> s.find('l')
2
>>> s[s.index('l'):]
'llo, world'
>>> s.rfind('l')
10
>>> s[:s.rindex('l')]
```

```
'Hello, wor'
>>> s[s.index('l'):s.rindex('l')]
'llo, wor'
```

Because Python strings accept negative subscripts, index is probably better used in situations like the one shown because using find instead would yield an unintended value.

replace

Replace works just like it sounds. It returns a copy of the string with all occurrences of the first parameter replaced with the second parameter.

```
>>> 'Hello, world'.replace('o', 'X')
'HellX, wXrld'
```

Or, using variable assignment:

```
string = 'Hello, world'
newString = string.replace('o', 'X')
print string
print newString
```

Outputs:

```
'Hello, world'
'HellX, wXrld'
```

Notice, the original variable (string) remains unchanged after the call to replace.

expandtabs

Replaces tabs with the appropriate number of spaces (default number of spaces per tab = 8; this can be changed by passing the tab size as an argument).

```
s = 'abcdefg\tabc\ta'
print s
print len(s)
t = s.expandtabs()
print t
print len(t)
```

Outputs:

```
abcdefg abc     a
13
abcdefg abc     a
17
```

Notice how (although these both look the same) the second string (t) has a different length because each tab is represented by spaces not tab characters.

To use a tab size of 4 instead of 8:

```
v = s.expandtabs(4)
print v
print len(v)
```

Outputs:

```
abcdefg abc a
13
```

Please note each tab is not always counted as eight spaces. Rather a tab "pushes" the count to the next multiple of eight. For example:

```
s = '\t\t'
print s.expandtabs().replace(' ', '*')
print len(s.expandtabs())
```

Output:

```
****************
16
```

```
s = 'abc\tabc\tabc'
print s.expandtabs().replace(' ', '*')
print len(s.expandtabs())
```

Outputs:

```
abc*****abc*****abc
19
```

split, splitlines

The **split** method returns a list of the words in the string. It can take a separator argument to use instead of whitespace.

```
>>> s = 'Hello, world'
>>> s.split()
['Hello,', 'world']
>>> s.split('l')
['He', '', 'o, wor', 'd']
```

Note that in neither case is the separator included in the split strings, but empty strings are allowed.

The **splitlines** method breaks a multiline string into many single line strings. It is analogous to split('\n') (but accepts '\r' and '\r\n' as delimiters as well) except that if the string ends in a newline character, **splitlines** ignores that final character (see example).

```
>>> s = """
... One line
... Two lines
... Red lines
... Blue lines
... Green lines
... """
>>> s.split('\n')
['', 'One line', 'Two lines', 'Red lines', 'Blue lines', 'Green lines',
'']
>>> s.splitlines()
['', 'One line', 'Two lines', 'Red lines', 'Blue lines', 'Green lines']
```

| Previous: Numbers | Index | Next: Lists |

Python Programming/Lists

| Previous: Strings | Index | Next: Tuples |

About lists in Python

A list in Python is an ordered group of items (or *elements*). It is a very general structure, and list elements don't have to be of the same type. For instance, you could put numbers, letters, strings and donkeys all on the same list.

If you are using a modern version of Python (and you should be), there is a class called 'list'. If you wish, you can make your own subclass of it, and determine list behaviour which is different than the default standard. But first, you should be familiar with the current behaviour of lists.

List notation

There are two different ways to make a list in python. The first is through assignment ("statically"), the second is using list comprehensions("actively").

To make a static list of items, write them between square brackets. For example:

```
[ 1,2,3,"This is a list",'c',Donkey("kong") ]
```

A couple of things to look at.

1. There are different data types here. Lists in python may contain more than one data type.
2. Objects can be created 'on the fly' and added to lists. The last item is a new kind of Donkey.

Writing lists this way is very quick (and obvious). However, it does not take into account the current state of anything else. The other way to make a list is to form it using list comprehension. That means you actually describe the process. To do that, the list is broken into two pieces. The first is a picture of what each element will look like, and the second is what you do to get it.

For instance, lets say we have a list of words:

```
listOfWords = ["this","is","a","list","of","words"]
```

We will take the first letter of each word and make a list out of it.

```
>>> listOfWords = ["this","is","a","list","of","words"]
>>> items = [ word[0] for word in listOfWords ]
>>> print items
['t', 'i', 'a', 'l', 'o', 'w']
```

List comprehension allows you to use more than one for statement. It will evaluate the items in all of the objects sequentially and will loop over the shorter objects if one object is longer than the rest.

```
>>> item = [x+y for x in 'flower' for y in 'pot']
>>> print item
['fp', 'fo', 'ft', 'lp', 'lo', 'lt', 'op', 'oo', 'ot', 'wp', 'wo',
'wt', 'ep', 'eo', 'et', 'rp', 'ro', 'rt']
```

Python's list comprehension does not define a scope. Any variables that are bound in an evaluation remain bound to whatever they were last bound to when the evaluation was completed:

```
>>> print x, y
r t
```

This is exactly the same as if the comprehension had been expanded into an explicitly-nested group of one or more 'for' statements and 0 or more 'if' statements.

List creation shortcuts

Python provides a shortcut to initialize a list to a particular size and with an initial value for each element:

```
>>> zeros=[0]*5
>>> print zeros
[0, 0, 0, 0, 0]
```

This works for any data type:

```
>>> foos=['foo']*8
>>> print foos
['foo', 'foo', 'foo', 'foo', 'foo', 'foo', 'foo', 'foo']
```

with a caveat. When building a new list by multiplying, Python copies each item by reference. This poses a problem for mutable items, for instance in a multidimensional array where each element is itself a list. You'd guess that the easy way to generate a two dimensional array would be:

```
listoflists=[ [0]*4 ] *5
```

and this works, but probably doesn't do what you expect:

```
>>> listoflists=[ [0]*4 ] *5
>>> print listoflists
[[0, 0, 0, 0], [0, 0, 0, 0], [0, 0, 0, 0], [0, 0, 0, 0], [0, 0, 0, 0]]
>>> listoflists[0][2]=1
>>> print listoflists
[[0, 0, 1, 0], [0, 0, 1, 0], [0, 0, 1, 0], [0, 0, 1, 0], [0, 0, 1, 0]]
```

What's happening here is that Python is using the same reference to the inner list as the elements of the outer list. Another way of looking at this issue is to examine how Python sees the above definition:

```
>>> innerlist=[0]*4
>>> listoflists=[innerlist]*5
>>> print listoflists
[[0, 0, 0, 0], [0, 0, 0, 0], [0, 0, 0, 0], [0, 0, 0, 0], [0, 0, 0, 0]]
>>> innerlist[2]=1
>>> print listoflists
[[0, 0, 1, 0], [0, 0, 1, 0], [0, 0, 1, 0], [0, 0, 1, 0], [0, 0, 1, 0]]
```

Assuming the above effect is not what you intend, one way around this issue is to use list comprehensions:

```
>>> listoflists=[[0]*4 for i in range(5)]
>>> print listoflists
[[0, 0, 0, 0], [0, 0, 0, 0], [0, 0, 0, 0], [0, 0, 0, 0], [0, 0, 0, 0]]
>>> listoflists[0][2]=1
```

```
>>> print listoflists
[[0, 0, 1, 0], [0, 0, 0, 0], [0, 0, 0, 0], [0, 0, 0, 0], [0, 0, 0, 0]]
```

Operations on lists

List Attributes

To find the length of a list use the built in len() method.

```
>>> len([1,2,3])
3
>>> a = [1,2,3,4]
>>> len( a )
4
```

Combining lists

Lists can be combined in several ways. The easiest is just to 'add' them. For instance:

```
>>> [1,2] + [3,4]
[1, 2, 3, 4]
```

Another way to combine lists is with **extend**. If you need to combine lists inside of a lambda, **extend** is the way to go.

```
>>> a = [1,2,3]
>>> b = [4,5,6]
>>> a.extend(b)
>>> print a
[1, 2, 3, 4, 5, 6]
```

The other way to append a value to a list is to use **append**. For example:

```
>>> p=[1,2]
>>> p.append([3,4])
>>> p
[1, 2, [3, 4]]
>>> # or
>>> print p
[1, 2, [3, 4]]
```

However, [3,4] is an element of the list, and not part of the list. **append** always adds one element only to the end of a list. So if the intention was to concatenate two lists, always use **extend**.

Getting pieces of lists (slices)

Continuous slices

Like strings, lists can be indexed and sliced.

```
>>> list = [2, 4, "usurp", 9.0,"n"]
>>> list[2]
'usurp'
>>> list[3:]
[9.0, 'n']
```

Much like the slice of a string is a substring, the slice of a list is a list. However, lists differ from strings in that we can assign new values to the items in a list.

```
>>> list[1] = 17
>>> list
[2, 17, 'usurp', 9.0,'n']
```

We can even assign new values to slices of the lists, which don't even have to be the same length

```
>>> list[1:4] = ["opportunistic", "elk"]
>>> list
[2, 'opportunistic', 'elk', 'n']
```

It's even possible to append things onto the end of lists by assigning to an empty slice:

```
>>> list[:0] = [3.14,2.71]
>>> list
[3.14, 2.71, 2, 'opportunistic', 'elk', 'n']
```

You can also completely change contents of a list:

```
>>> list[:] = ['new', 'list', 'contents']
>>> list
['new', 'list', 'contents']
```

On the right site of assign statement can be any iterable type:

```
>>> list[:2] = ('element',('t',),[])
>>> list
['element', ('t',), [], 'contents']
```

With slicing you can create copy of list because slice returns a new list:

```
>>> original = [1, 'element', []]
>>> list_copy = original[:]
>>> list_copy
[1, 'element', []]
>>> list_copy.append('new element')
>>> list_copy
[1, 'element', [], 'new element']
>>> original
[1, 'element', []]
```

but this is shallow copy and contains references to elements from original list, so be careful with mutable types:

```
>>> list_copy[2].append('something')
>>> original
[1, 'element', ['something']]
```

Non-Continuous slices

It is also possible to get non-continuous parts of an array. If one wanted to get every n-th occurrence of a list, one would use the :: operator. The syntax is a:b:n where a and b are the start and end of the slice to be operated upon.

```
>>> list = [i for i in range(10) ]
>>> list[::2]
[0, 2, 4, 6, 8]
>>> list[1:7:2]
[1, 3, 5]
```

Comparing lists

Lists can be compared for equality.

```
>>> [1,2] == [1,2]
True
>>> [1,2] == [3,4]
False
```

Sorting lists

Sorting lists is easy with a sort method.

```
>>> list = [2, 3, 1, 'a', 'b']
>>> list.sort()
>>> list
[1, 2, 3, 'a', 'b']
```

Note that the list is sorted in place, and the sort() method returns **None** to emphasize this side effect.

If you use Python 2.4 or higher there are some more sort parameters:

sort(cmp,key,reverse)

cmp : method to be used for sorting

key : function to be executed with key element. List is sorted by return-value of the function

reverse : sort ascending y/n

List methods

append(x)

Add item *x* onto the end of the list.

```
>>> list = [1, 2, 3]
>>> list.append(4)
>>> list
[1, 2, 3, 4]
```

See pop(i)

pop(i)

Remove the item in the list at the index *i* and return it. If *i* is not given, remove the the last item in the list and return it.

```
>>> list = [1, 2, 3, 4]
>>> a = list.pop(0)
>>> list
[2, 3, 4]
>>> a
1
>>> b = list.pop()
>>>list
[2, 3]
>>> b
4
```

| Previous: Strings | Index | Next: Tuples |

Python Programming/Tuples

| Previous: Lists | Index | Next: Dictionaries |

About tuples in Python

A tuple in Python is much like a list except that it is immutable (unchangeable) once created. They are generally used for data which should not be edited.

Tuple notation

Tuples may be created directly or converted from lists. Generally, tuples are enclosed in parenthesis.

```
>>> l = [1, 'a', [6, 3.14]]
>>> t = (1, 'a', [6, 3.14])
>>> t
(1, 'a', [6, 3.1400000000000001])
>>> tuple(l)
(1, 'a', [6, 3.1400000000000001])
>>> t == tuple(l)
True
>>> t == l
False
```

A one item tuple is created by a item in parens followed by a comma:

```
>>> t = ('A single item tuple',)
>>> t
('A single item tuple',)
```

Also, tuples will be created from items separated by commas.

```
>>> t = 'A', 'tuple', 'needs', 'no', 'parens'
>>> t
('A', 'tuple', 'needs', 'no', 'parens')
```

Packing and Unpacking

You can also perform multiple assignment using tuples.

```
>>> article, noun, verb, adjective, direct_object = t
>>> noun
'tuple'
```

Note that either, or both sides of an assignment operator can consist of tuples.

```
>>> a, b = 1, 2
>>> b
2
```

Assigning a tuple to a several different variables is called "tuple unpacking," while assigning multiple values to a tuple in one variable is called "tuple packing." When unpacking a tuple, or performing multiple assignment, you must have the same number of variables being assigned to as values being assigned.

Operations on tuples

These are the same as for lists except that we may not assign to indices or slices, and there is no "append" operator.

```
>>> a = (1, 2)
>>> b = (3, 4)
>>> a + b
(1, 2, 3, 4)
>>> a
(1, 2)
>>> b
(3, 4)
>>> print a.append(3)
Traceback (most recent call last):
File "<stdin>", line 1, in ?
AttributeError: 'tuple' object has no attribute 'append'
>>> a
(1, 2)
>>> a[0] = 0
Traceback (most recent call last):
File "<stdin>", line 1, in ?
TypeError: object does not support item assignment
>>> a
(1, 2)
```

For lists we would have had:

```
>>> a = [1, 2]
>>> b = [3, 4]
```

```
>>> a + b
[1, 2, 3, 4]
>>> a
[1, 2]
>>> b
[3, 4]
>>> a.append(3)
>>> a
[1, 2, 3]
>>> a[0] = 0
>>> a
[0, 2, 3]
```

Tuple Attributes

Length: Finding the length of a tuple is the same as with lists; use the built in len() method.

```
>>> len( ( 1, 2, 3) )
3
>>> a = ( 1, 2, 3, 4 )
>>> len( a )
4
```

Conversions

Convert list to tuples using the built in tuple() method.

```
>>> l = [4, 5, 6]
>>> tuple(l)
(4, 5, 6)
```

Converting a tuple into a list using the built in list() method to cast as a list:

```
>>> t = (4, 5, 6)
>>> list(t)
[4, 5, 6]
```

Dictionaries can also be converted to tuples of tuples using the items method of dictionaries:

```
>>> d = {'a': 1, 'b': 2}
>>> tuple(d.items())
(('a', 1), ('b', 2))
```

Uses of Tuples

Tuples can be used like lists and are appropriate when a list may be used but the size is known and small. One very useful situation is returning multiple values from a function. To return multiple values in many other languages requires creating an object or container of some type, but in Python it is easy:

```
def func(x,y):
    # code to compute a and b
    return (a,b)
```

This can be combined with the unpacking technique above in later code to retrieve both return values:

```
(a,b) = func(1,2)
```

Previous: Lists	Index	Next: Dictionaries

Python Programming/Dictionaries

Previous: Tuples	Index	Next: Sets

About dictionaries in Python

A dictionary in python is a collection of unordered values which are accessed by key.

Dictionary notation

Dictionaries may be created directly or converted from sequences. Dictionaries are enclosed in curly braces, { }

```
>>> d = {'city':'Paris', 'age':38, (102,1650,1601):'A matrix coordinate'}
>>> seq = [('city','Paris'), ('age', 38), ((102,1650,1601),'A matrix
coordinate')]
>>> d
{'city': 'Paris', 'age': 38, (102, 1650, 1601): 'A matrix coordinate'}
>>> dict(seq)
{'city': 'Paris', 'age': 38, (102, 1650, 1601): 'A matrix coordinate'}
>>> d == dict(seq)
True
```

Also, dictionaries can be easily created by zipping two sequences.

```
>>> seq1 = ('a','b','c','d')
>>> seq2 = [1,2,3,4]
>>> d = dict(zip(seq1,seq2))
>>> d
{'a': 1, 'c': 3, 'b': 2, 'd': 4}
```

Operations on Dictionaries

The operations on dictionaries are somewhat unique. Slicing is not supported, since the items have no intrinsic order.

```
>>> d = {'a':1,'b':2, 'cat':'Fluffers'}
>>> d.keys()
['a', 'b', 'cat']
>>> d.values()
[1, 2, 'Fluffers']
>>> d['a']
1
>>> d['cat'] = 'Mr. Whiskers'
>>> d['cat']
'Mr. Whiskers'
```

```
>>> 'cat' in d
True
>>> 'dog' in d
False
```

Combining two Dictionaries

You can combine two dictionaries by using the update method of the primary dictionary. Note that the update method will merge existing elements if they conflict.

```
>>> d = {'apples': 1, 'oranges': 3, 'pears': 2}
>>> ud = {'pears': 4, 'grapes': 5, 'lemons': 6}
>>> d.update(ud)
>>> d
{'grapes': 5, 'pears': 4, 'lemons': 6, 'apples': 1, 'oranges': 3}
>>>
```

Deleting from dictionary

```
del dictionaryName[membername]
```

Previous: Tuples	Index	Next: Sets

Python Programming/Sets

Previous: Dictionaries	Index	Next: Operators

Python also has an implementation of the mathematical set. Unlike sequence objects such as lists and tuples, in which each element is indexed, a set is an unordered collection of objects. Sets also cannot have duplicate members - a given object appears in a set 0 or 1 times. For more information on sets, see the Set Theory wikibook. Sets also require that all members of the set be hashable. Any object that can be used as a dictionary key can be a set member. Integers, floating point numbers, tuples, and strings are hashable; dictionaries, lists, and other sets (except frozensets) are not.

Constructing Sets

One way to construct sets is by passing any sequential object to the "set" constructor.

```
>>> set([0, 1, 2, 3])
set([0, 1, 2, 3])
>>> set("obtuse")
set(['b', 'e', 'o', 's', 'u', 't'])
```

We can also add elements to sets one by one, using the "add" function.

```
>>> s = set([12, 26, 54])
>>> s.add(32)
>>> s
set([32, 26, 12, 54])
```

Note that since a set does not contain duplicate elements, if we add one of the members of s to s again, the add function will have no effect. This same behavior occurs in the "update" function, which adds a group of elements to a set.

```
>>> s.update([26, 12, 9, 14])
>>> s
set([32, 9, 12, 14, 54, 26])
```

Note that you can give any type of sequential structure, or even another set, to the update function, regardless of what structure was used to initialize the set.

The set function also provides a copy constructor. However, remember that the copy constructor will copy the set, but not the individual elements.

```
>>> s2 = s.copy()
>>> s2
set([32, 9, 12, 14, 54, 26])
```

Membership Testing

We can check if an object is in the set using the same "in" operator as with sequential data types.

```
>>> 32 in s
True
>>> 6 in s
False
>>> 6 not in s
True
```

We can also test the membership of entire sets. Given two sets S_1 and S_2, we check if S_1 is a subset or a superset of S_2.

```
>>> s.issubset(set([32, 8, 9, 12, 14, -4, 54, 26, 19]))
True
>>> s.issuperset(set([9, 12]))
True
```

Note that "issubset" and "issuperset" can also accept sequential data types as arguments

```
>>> s.issuperset([32, 9])
True
```

Note that the <= and >= operators also express the issubset and issuperset functions respectively.

```
>>> set([4, 5, 7]) <= set([4, 5, 7, 9])
True
>>> set([9, 12, 15]) >= set([9, 12])
True
```

Like lists, tuples, and string, we can use the "len" function to find the number of items in a set.

Removing Items

There are three functions which remove individual items from a set, called pop, remove, and discard. The first, pop, simply removes an item from the set. Note that there is no defined behavior as to which element it chooses to remove.

```
>>> s = set([1,2,3,4,5,6])
>>> s.pop()
1
>>> s
set([2,3,4,5,6])
```

We also have the "remove" function to remove a specified element.

```
>>> s.remove(3)
>>> s
set([2,4,5,6])
```

However, removing a item which isn't in the set causes an error.

```
>>> s.remove(9)
Traceback (most recent call last):
  File "<stdin>", line 1, in ?
KeyError: 9
```

If you wish to avoid this error, use "discard." It has the same functionality as remove, but will simply do nothing if the element isn't in the set

We also have another operation for removing elements from a set, clear, which simply removes all elements from the set.

```
>>> s.clear()
>>> s
set([])
```

Iteration Over Sets

We can also have a loop move over each of the items in a set. However, since sets are unordered, it is undefined which order the iteration will follow.

```
>>> s = set("blerg")
>>> for n in s:
...     print n,
...
r b e l g
```

Set Operations

Python allows us to perform all the standard mathematical set operations, using members of set. Note that each of these set operations has several forms. One of these forms, s1.function(s2) will return another set which is created by "function" applied to S_1 and S_2. The other form, s1.function_update(s2), will change S_1 to be the set created by "function" of S_1 and S_2. Finally, some functions have equivalent special operators. For example, s1 & s2 is equivalent to s1.intersection(s2)

Union

The union is the merger of two sets. Any element in S_1 or S_2 will appear in their union.

```
>>> s1 = set([4, 6, 9])
>>> s2 = set([1, 6, 8])
>>> s1.union(s2)
set([1, 4, 6, 8, 9])
>>> s1 | s2
set([1, 4, 6, 8, 9])
```

Note that union's update function is simply "update" above.

Intersection

Any element which is in both S_1 and S_2 will appear in their intersection.

```
>>> s1 = set([4, 6, 9])
>>> s2 = set([1, 6, 8])
>>> s1.intersection(s2)
set([6])
>>> s1 & s2
set([6])
>>> s1.intersection_update(s2)
>>> s1
set([6])
```

Symmetric Difference

The symmetric difference of two sets is the set of elements which are in one of either set, but not in both.

```
>>> s1 = set([4, 6, 9])
>>> s2 = set([1, 6, 8])
>>> s1.symmetric_difference(s2)
set([8, 1, 4, 9])
>>> s1 ^ s2
set([8, 1, 4, 9])
>>> s1.symmetric_difference_update(s2)
>>> s1
set([8, 1, 4, 9])
```

Set Difference

Python can also find the set difference of S_1 and S_2, which is the elements that are in S_1 but not in S_2.

```
>>> s1 = set([4, 6, 9])
>>> s2 = set([1, 6, 8])
>>> s1.difference(s2)
set([9, 4])
>>> s1 - s2
set([9, 4])
>>> s1.difference_update(s2)
>>> s1
set([9, 4])
```

frozenset

A frozenset is basically the same as a set, except that it is immutable - once it is created, its members cannot be changed. Since they are immutable, they are also hashable, which means that frozensets can be used as members in other sets and as dictionary keys. frozensets have the same functions as normal sets, except none of the functions that change the contents (update, remove, pop, etc.) are available.

```
>>> fs = frozenset([2, 3, 4])
>>> s1 = set([fs, 4, 5, 6])
>>> s1
set([4, frozenset([2, 3, 4]), 6, 5])
>>> fs.intersection(s1)
frozenset([4])
>>> fs.add(6)
Traceback (most recent call last):
  File "<stdin>", line 1, in <module>
AttributeError: 'frozenset' object has no attribute 'add'
```

Reference

Python Library Reference on Set Types [1]

Previous: Dictionaries	Index	Next: Operators

References

[1] http://python.org/doc/2.5.2/lib/types-set.html

Python Programming/Operators

| Previous: Sets | Index | Next: Flow control |

Basics

Python math works like you would expect.

```
>>> x = 2
>>> y = 3
>>> z = 5
>>> x * y
6
>>> x + y
5
>>> x * y + z
11
>>> (x + y) * z
25
```

Note that Python adheres to the PEMDAS order of operations.

Powers

There is a built in exponentiation operator **, which can take either integers, floating point or complex numbers. This occupies its proper place in the order of operations.

```
>>> 2**8
256
```

Division and Type Conversion

For Python 2.x, dividing two integers or longs uses integer division, also known as "floor division" (applying the floor function after division. So, for example, 5 / 2 is 2. Using "/" to do division this way is deprecated; if you want floor division, use "//" (available in Python 2.2 and later).

"/" does "true division" for floats and complex numbers; for example, 5.0/2.0 is 2.5.

For Python 3.x, "/" does "true division" for all types.[1] [2]

Dividing by or into a floating point number (there are no fractional types in Python) will cause Python to use true division. To coerce an integer to become a float, 'float()' with the integer as a parameter

```
>>> x = 5
>>> float(x)
5.0
```

This can be generalized for other numeric types: int(), complex(), long().

Beware that due to the limitations of floating point arithmetic, rounding errors can cause unexpected results. For example:

```
>>> print 0.6/0.2
3.0
>>> print 0.6//0.2
2.0
```

Modulo

The modulus (remainder of the division of the two operands, rather than the quotient) can be found using the % operator, or by the divmod builtin function. The divmod function returns a tuple containing the quotient and remainder.

```
>>> 10%7
3
```

Negation

Unlike some other languages, variables can be negated directly:

```
>>> x = 5
>>> -x
-5
```

Augmented Assignment

There is shorthand for assigning the output of an operation to one of the inputs:

```
>>> x = 2
>>> x  # 2
2
>>> x *= 3
>>> x  # 2 * 3
6
>>> x += 4
>>> x  # 2 * 3 + 4
10
>>> x /= 5
>>> x  # (2 * 3 + 4) / 5
2
>>> x **= 2
>>> x  # ((2 * 3 + 4) / 5) ** 2
4
>>> x %= 3
>>> x  # ((2 * 3 + 4) / 5) ** 2 % 3
1

>>> x = 'repeat this  '
>>> x   # repeat this
repeat this
>>> x *= 3   # fill with x repeated three times
>>> x
```

```
repeat this   repeat this   repeat this
```

Boolean

or:

```
if a or b:
    do_this
else:
    do_this
```

and:

```
if a and b:
    do_this
else:
    do_this
```

not:

```
if not a:
    do_this
else:
    do_this
```

Previous: Sets	Index	Next: Flow control

References

[1] [http://www.python.org/doc/2.2.3/whatsnew/node7.html What's New in Python 2.2

[2] PEP 238 -- Changing the Division Operator (http://www.python.org/dev/peps/pep-0238/)

Python Programming/Flow control

Previous: Operators	Index	Next: Functions

As with most imperative languages, there are three main categories of program flow control:

- loops
- branches
- function calls

Function calls are covered in the next section.

Generators and list comprehensions are advanced forms of program flow control, but they are not covered here.

Loops

In Python, there are two kinds of loops, 'for' loops and 'while' loops.

For loops

A for loop iterates over elements of a sequence (tuple or list). A variable is created to represent the object in the sequence. For example,

```
l = [100,200,300,400]
for i in l:
    print i
```

This will output

```
100
200
300
400
```

The for loop loops over each of the elements of a list or iterator, assigning the current element to the variable name given. In the first example above, each of the elements in l is assigned to i.

A builtin function called range exists to make creating sequential lists such as the one above easier. The loop above is equivalent to:

```
l = range(100, 401,100)
for i in l:
    print i
```

The next example uses a negative *step* (the third argument for the built-in range function):

```
for i in range(10, 0, -1):
    print i
```

This will output

```
10
9
8
7
```

```
6
5
4
3
2
1
```

or

```
for i in range(10, 0, -2):
    print i
```

This will output

```
10
8
6
4
2
```

for loops can have names for each element of a tuple, if it loops over a sequence of tuples. For instance

```
l = [(1, 1), (2, 4), (3, 9), (4, 16), (5, 25)]
for x, xsquared in l:
    print x, ':', xsquared
```

will output

```
1 : 1
2 : 4
3 : 9
4 : 16
5 : 25
```

While loops

A while loop repeats a sequence of statements until some condition becomes false. For example:

```
x = 5
while x > 0:
    print x
    x = x - 1
```

Will output:

```
5
4
3
2
1
```

Python's while loops can also have an 'else' clause, which is a block of statements that is executed (once) when the while statement evaluates to false. The break statement inside the while loop will not direct the program flow to the else clause. For example:

```
x = 5
y = x
while y > 0:
    print y
    y = y - 1
else:
    print x
```

This will output:

```
5
4
3
2
1
5
```

Unlike some languages, there is no post-condition loop.

Breaking, continuing and the else clause of loops

Python includes statements to exit a loop (either a for loop or a while loop) prematurely. To exit a loop, use the break statement

```
x = 5
while x > 0:
    print x
    break
    x -= 1
    print x
```

this will output

```
5
```

The statement to begin the next iteration of the loop without waiting for the end of the current loop is 'continue'.

```
l = [5,6,7]
for x in l:
    continue
    print x
```

This will not produce any output.

The else clause of loops will be executed if no break statements are met in the loop.

```
l = range(1,100)
for x in l:
    if x == 100:
        print x
        break
    else:
        print x," is not 100"
else:
```

```
    print "100 not found in range"
```

Another example of a while loop using the break statement and the else statement:

```
expected_str = "melon"
received_str = "apple"
basket = ["banana", "grapes", "strawberry", "melon", "orange"]
x = 0
step = int(raw_input("Input iteration step: "))

while(received_str != expected_str):
    if(x >= len(basket)): print "No more fruits left on the basket.";
break
    received_str = basket[x]
    x += step # Change this to 3 to make the while statement
              # evaluate to false, avoiding the break statement, using
the else clause.
    if(received_str==basket[2]): print "I hate",basket[2],"!"; break
    if(received_str != expected_str): print "I am waiting for my
",expected_str,"."
else:
    print "Finally got what I wanted! my precious ",expected_str,"!"
print "Going back home now !"
```

This will output:

```
Input iteration step: 2
I am waiting for my  melon .
I hate strawberry !
Going back home now !
```

Branches

There is basically only one kind of branch in Python, the 'if' statement. The simplest form of the if statement simple executes a block of code only if a given predicate is true, and skips over it if the predicate is false

For instance,

```
>>> x = 10
>>> if x > 0:
...     print "Positive"
...
Positive
>>> if x < 0:
...     print "Negative"
...
```

You can also add "elif" (short for "else if") branches onto the if statement. If the predicate on the first "if" is false, it will test the predicate on the first elif, and run that branch if it's true. If the first elif is false, it tries the second one, and so on. Note, however, that it will stop checking branches as soon as it finds a true predicate, and skip the rest of the if statement. You can also end your if statements with an "else" branch. If none of the other branches are executed, then python will run this branch.

```
>>> x = -6
>>> if x > 0:
...     print "Positive"
... elif x == 0:
...     print "Zero"
... else:
...     print "Negative"
...
'Negative'
```

Conclusion

Any of these loops, branches, and function calls can be nested in any way desired. A loop can loop over a loop, a branch can branch again, and a function can call other functions, or even call itself.

Previous: Operators	Index	Next: Functions

Python Programming/Functions

Previous: Flow control	Index	Next: Decorators

Function calls

A *callable object* is an object that can accept some arguments (also called parameters) and possibly return an object (often a tuple containing multiple objects).

A function is the simplest callable object in Python, but there are others, such as classes or certain class instances.

Defining functions

A function is defined in Python by the following format:

```
def functionname(arg1, arg2, ...):
    statement1
    statement2
    ...
```

```
>>> def functionname(arg1,arg2):
...     return arg1+arg2
...
>>> t = functionname(24,24) # Result: 48
```

If a function takes no arguments, it must still include the parentheses, but without anything in them:

```
def functionname():
    statement1
    statement2
    ...
```

The arguments in the function definition bind the arguments passed at function invocation (i.e. when the function is called), which are called actual parameters, to the names given when the function is defined, which are called formal parameters. The interior of the function has no knowledge of the names given to the actual parameters; the names of the actual parameters may not even be accessible (they could be inside another function).

A function can 'return' a value, like so

```
def square(x):
    return x*x
```

A function can define variables within the function body, which are considered 'local' to the function. The locals together with the arguments comprise all the variables within the scope of the function. Any names within the function are unbound when the function returns or reaches the end of the function body.

Declaring Arguments

Default Argument Values

If any of the formal parameters in the function definition are declared with the format "arg = value," then you will have the option of not specifying a value for those arguments when calling the function. If you do not specify a value, then that parameter will have the default value given when the function executes.

```
>>> def display_message(message, truncate_after = 4):
...     print message[:truncate_after]
...
>>> display_message("message")
mess
>>> display_message("message", 6)
messag
```

Variable-Length Argument Lists

Python allows you to declare two special arguments which allow you to create arbitrary-length argument lists. This means that each time you call the function, you can specify any number of arguments above a certain number.

```
def function(first,second,*remaining):
    statement1
    statement2
    ...
```

When calling the above function, you must provide value for each of the first two arguments. However, since the third parameter is marked with an asterisk, any actual parameters after the first two will be packed into a tuple and bound to "remaining."

```
>>> def print_tail(first,*tail):
...     print tail
...
>>> print_tail(1, 5, 2, "omega")
(5, 2, 'omega')
```

If we declare a formal parameter prefixed with *two* asterisks, then it will be bound to a dictionary containing any keyword arguments in the actual parameters which do not correspond to any formal parameters. For example, consider the function:

```
def make_dictionary(max_length = 10, **entries):
    return dict([(key, entries[key]) for i, key in
enumerate(entries.keys()) if i < max_length])
```

If we call this function with any keyword arguments other than max_length, they will be placed in the dictionary "entries." If we include the keyword argument of max_length, it will be bound to the formal parameter max_length, as usual.

```
>>> make_dictionary(max_length = 2, key1 = 5, key2 = 7, key3 = 9)
{'key3': 9, 'key2': 7}
```

Calling functions

A function can be called by appending the arguments in parentheses to the function name, or an empty matched set of parentheses if the function takes no arguments.

```
foo()
square(3)
bar(5, x)
```

A function's return value can be used by assigning it to a variable, like so:

```
x = foo()
y = bar(5,x)
```

As shown above, when calling a function you can specify the parameters by name and you can do so in any order

```
def display_message(message, start=0, end=4):
    print message[start:end]

display_message("message", end=3)
```

This above is valid and start will be the default value of 0. A restriction placed on this is after the first named argument then all arguments after it must also be named. The following is not valid

```
display_message(end=5, start=1, "my message")
```

because the third argument ("my message") is an unnamed argument.

Closure

Closure, also known as nested function definition, is a function defined inside another function. Perhaps best described with an example:

```
>>> def outer(outer_argument):
...     def inner(inner_argument):
...         return outer_argument + inner_argument
...     return inner
...
>>> f = outer(5)
>>> f(3)
8
>>> f(4)
9
```

Closure is possible in python because function is a first-class object, that means a function is merely an object of type function. Being an object means it is possible to pass function object (an uncalled function) around as argument or as return value or to assign another name to the function object. A unique feature that makes closure useful is that the enclosed function may use the names defined in the parent function's scope.

lambda

lambda is an anonymous (unnamed) function, it is used primarily to write very short functions that is a hassle to define in the normal way. A function like this:

```
>>> def add(a, b):
...     return a + b
...
>>> add(4, 3)
7
```

may also be defined using lambda

```
>>> print (lambda a, b: a + b)(4, 3)
7
```

Lambda is often used as an argument to other functions that expects a function object, such as sorted()'s 'key' argument.

```
>>> sorted([[3, 4], [3, 5], [1, 2], [7, 3]], key=lambda x: x[1])
[[1, 2], [7, 3], [3, 4], [3, 5]]
```

The lambda form is often useful to be used as closure, such as illustrated in the following example:

```
>>> def attribution(name):
...     return lambda x: x + ' -- ' + name
...
>>> pp = attribution('John')
>>> pp('Dinner is in the fridge')
'Dinner is in the fridge -- John'
```

note that the lambda function can use the values of variables from the scope in which it was created (like pre and post). This is the essence of closure.

| Previous: Flow control | Index | Next: Decorators |

Python Programming/Decorators

Previous: Functions	Index	Next: Scoping

Decorator in Python is a syntax sugar for high-level function.

Minimal Example of property decorator:

```
>>> class Foo(object):
...     @property
...     def bar(self):
...         return 'baz'
...
>>> F = Foo()
>>> print F.bar
baz
```

The above example is really just a syntax sugar for codes like this:

```
>>> class Foo(object):
...     def bar(self):
...         return 'baz'
...     bar = property(bar)
...
>>> F = Foo()
>>> print F.bar
baz
```

Minimal Example of generic decorator:

```
>>> def decorator(f):
...     def called(*args, **kargs):
...         print 'A function is called somewhere'
...         return f(*args, **kargs)
...     return called
...
>>> class Foo(object):
...     @decorator
...     def bar(self):
...         return 'baz'
...
>>> F = Foo()
>>> print F.bar()
A function is called somewhere
baz
```

A good use for the decorators is to allow you to refactor your code so that common features can be moved into decorators. Consider for example, that you would like to trace all calls to some functions and print out the values of all the parameters of the functions for each invocation. Now you can implement this in a decorator as follows

```
#define the Trace class that will be
#invoked using decorators
class Trace(object):
    def __init__(self, f):
        self.f =f

    def __call__(self, *args, **kwds):
        print "entering function " + self.f.__name__
        i=0
        for arg in args:
            print "arg {0}: {1}".format(i, arg)
            i =i+1

        return self.f(*args, **kwds)
```

Then you can use the decorator on any function that you defined by

```
@Trace
def sum(a, b):
    print "inside sum"
    return a + b
```

On running this code you would see output like

```
>>> sum(3,2)
entering function sum
arg 0: 3
arg 1: 2
inside sum
```

Alternately instead of creating the decorator as a class you could have use a function as well.

```
def Trace(f):
    def my_f(*args, **kwds):
        print "entering " +   f.__name__
        result= f(*args, **kwds)
        print "exiting " +   f.__name__
        return result
    my_f.__name = f.__name__
    my_f.__doc__ = f.__doc__
    return my_f

#An example of the trace decorator
@Trace
def sum(a, b):
    print "inside sum"
    return a + b


if you run this you should see
>>> sum(3,2)
```

```
entering sum
inside sum
exiting sum
10: 5
```

remember it is good practice to return the function or a sensible decorated replacement for the function. So that decorators can be chained.

Previous: Functions	Index	Next: Scoping

Python Programming/Scoping

Previous: Decorators	Index	Next: Exceptions

Variables

Variables in Python are automatically declared by assignment. Variables are always references to objects, and are never typed. Variables exist only in the current scope or global scope. When they go out of scope, the variables are destroyed, but the objects to which they refer are not (unless the number of references to the object drops to zero).

Scope is delineated by function and class blocks. Both functions and their scopes can be nested. So therefore

```
def foo():
    def bar():
        x = 5 # x is now in scope
        return x + y # y is defined in the enclosing scope later
    y = 10
    return bar() # now that y is defined, bar's scope includes y
```

Now when this code is tested,

```
>>> foo()
15
>>> bar()
Traceback (most recent call last):
  File "<pyshell#26>", line 1, in -toplevel-
    bar()
NameError: name 'bar' is not defined
```

The name 'bar' is not found because a higher scope does not have access to the names lower in the hierarchy.

It is a common pitfall to fail to lookup an attribute (such as a method) of an object (such as a container) referenced by a variable before the variable is assigned the object. In its most common form:

```
>>> for x in range(10):
        y.append(x) # append is an attribute of lists


Traceback (most recent call last):
  File "<pyshell#46>", line 2, in -toplevel-
```

```
    y.append(x)
NameError: name 'y' is not defined
```

Here, to correct this problem, one must add y = [] before the for loop.

Previous: Decorators	Index	Next: Exceptions

Python Programming/Exceptions

Previous: Scoping	Index	Next: Input and output

Python handles all errors with exceptions.

An *exception* is a signal that an error or other unusual condition has occurred. There are a number of built-in exceptions, which indicate conditions like reading past the end of a file, or dividing by zero. You can also define your own exceptions.

Raising exceptions

Whenever your program attempts to do something erroneous or meaningless, Python raises exception to such conduct:

```
>>> 1 / 0
Traceback (most recent call last):
  File "<stdin>", line 1, in ?
ZeroDivisionError: integer division or modulo by zero
```

This *traceback* indicates that the ZeroDivisionError exception is being raised. This is a built-in exception -- see below for a list of all the other ones.

Catching exceptions

In order to handle errors, you can set up *exception handling blocks* in your code. The keywords try and except are used to catch exceptions. When an error occurs within the try block, Python looks for a matching except block to handle it. If there is one, execution jumps there.

If you execute this code:

```
try:
    print 1/0
except ZeroDivisionError:
    print "You can't divide by zero, you silly."
```

Then Python will print this:

```
You can't divide by zero, you silly.
```

If you don't specify an exception type on the except line, it will cheerfully catch all exceptions. This is generally a bad idea in production code, since it means your program will blissfully ignore *unexpected* errors as well as ones which the except block is actually prepared to handle.

Exceptions can propagate up the call stack:

```
def f(x):
    return g(x) + 1

def g(x):
    if x < 0: raise ValueError, "I can't cope with a negative number here."
    else: return 5

try:
    print f(-6)
except ValueError:
    print "That value was invalid."
```

In this code, the print statement calls the function f. That function calls the function g, which will raise an exception of type ValueError. Neither f nor g has a try/except block to handle ValueError. So the exception raised propagates out to the main code, where there *is* an exception-handling block waiting for it. This code prints:

```
That value was invalid.
```

Sometimes it is useful to find out exactly what went wrong, or to print the python error text yourself. For example:

```
try:
    the_file = open("the_parrot")
except IOError, (ErrorNumber, ErrorMessage):
    if ErrorNumber == 2: # file not found
        print "Sorry, 'the_parrot' has apparently joined the choir
invisible."
    else:
        print "Congratulation! you have managed to trip a #%d error" %
ErrorNumber  # String concatenation is slow, use % formatting whenever
possible
        print ErrorMessage
```

Which of course will print:

```
Sorry, 'the_parrot' has apparently joined the choir invisible.
```

Custom Exceptions

Code similar to that seen above can be used to create custom exceptions and pass information along with them. This can be extremely useful when trying to debug complicated projects. Here is how that code would look; first creating the custom exception class:

```
class CustomException(Exception):
    def __init__(self, value):
        self.parameter = value
    def __str__(self):
        return repr(self.parameter)
```

And then using that exception:

```
try:
    raise CustomException("My Useful Error Message")
except CustomException, (instance):
```

```
    print "Caught: " + instance.parameter
```

Recovering and continuing with finally

Exceptions could lead to a situation where, after raising an exception, the code block where the exception occurred might not be revisited. In some cases this might leave external resources used by the program in an unknown state.

finally clause allows programmers to close such resources in case of an exception. Between 2.4 and 2.5 version of python there is change of syntax for finally clause.

- Python 2.4

```
try:
    result = None
    try:
        result = x/y
    except ZeroDivisionError:
        print "division by zero!"
    print "result is ", result
finally:
    print "executing finally clause"
```

- Python 2.5

```
try:
    result = x / y
except ZeroDivisionError:
    print "division by zero!"
else:
    print "result is", result
finally:
    print "executing finally clause"
```

Built-in exception classes

All built-in Python exceptions [1]

Exotic uses of exceptions

Exceptions are good for more than just error handling. If you have a complicated piece of code to choose which of several courses of action to take, it can be useful to use exceptions to jump out of the code as soon as the decision can be made. The Python-based mailing list software Mailman does this in deciding how a message should be handled. Using exceptions like this may seem like it's a sort of GOTO -- and indeed it is, but a limited one called an *escape continuation*. Continuations are a powerful functional-programming tool and it can be useful to learn them.

Just as a simple example of how exceptions make programming easier, say you want to add items to a list but you don't want to use "if" statements to initialize the list we could replace this:

```
if hasattr(self, 'items'):
    self.items.extend(new_items)
else:
    self.items = list(new_items)
```

Using exceptions, we can emphasize the normal program flow—that usually we just extend the list—rather than emphasizing the unusual case:

```
try:
    self.items.extend(new_items)
except AttributeError:
    self.items = list(new_items)
```

Previous: Scoping	Index	Next: Input and output

References

[1] http://docs.python.org/library/exceptions.html

Python Programming/Input and output

Previous: Exceptions	Index	Next: Modules

Input

Python has two functions designed for accepting data directly from the user:

- input()
- raw_input()

There are also very simple ways of reading a file and, for stricter control over input, reading from stdin if necessary.

raw_input()

raw_input() asks the user for a string of data (ended with a newline), and simply returns the string. It can also take an argument, which is displayed as a prompt before the user enters the data. E.g.

```
print raw_input('What is your name? ')
```

prints out

```
What is your name? <user input data here>
```

Note: in 3.x "...raw_input() was renamed to input(). That is, the new input() function reads a line from sys.stdin and returns it with the trailing newline stripped. It raises EOFError if the input is terminated prematurely. To get the old behavior of input(), use eval(input())."

input()

input() uses raw_input to read a string of data, and then attempts to evaluate it as if it were a Python program, and then returns the value that results. So entering

```
[1,2,3]
```

would return a list containing those numbers, just as if it were assigned directly in the Python script.

More complicated expressions are possible. For example, if a script says:

```
x = input('What are the first 10 perfect squares? ')
```

it is possible for a user to input:

```
map(lambda x: x*x, range(10))
```

which yields the correct answer in list form. Note that no inputted statement can span more than one line.

input() should not be used for anything but the most trivial program. Turning the strings returned from raw_input() into python types using an idiom such as:

```
x = None
while not x:
    try:
        x = int(raw_input())
    except ValueError:
        print 'Invalid Number'
```

is preferable, as input() uses eval() to turn a literal into a python type. This will allow a malicious person to run arbitrary code from inside your program trivially.

File Input

File Objects

Python includes a built-in file type. Files can be opened by using the file type's constructor:

```
f = file('test.txt', 'r')
```

This means f is open for reading. The first argument is the filename and the second parameter is the mode, which can be 'r', 'w', or 'rw', among some others.

The most common way to read from a file is simply to iterate over the lines of the file:

```
f = open('test.txt', 'r')
for line in f:
    print line[0]
f.close()
```

This will print the first character of each line. Note that a newline is attached to the end of each line read this way.

Because files are automatically closed when the file object goes out of scope, there is no real need to close them explicitly. So, the loop in the previous code can also be written as:

```
for line in open('test.txt', 'r'):
    print line[0]
```

It is also possible to read limited numbers of characters at a time, like so:

```
c = f.read(1)
while len(c) > 0:
    if len(c.strip()) > 0: print c,
    c = f.read(1)
```

This will read the characters from f one at a time, and then print them if they're not whitespace.

A file object implicitly contains a marker to represent the current position. If the file marker should be moved back to the beginning, one can either close the file object and reopen it or just move the marker back to the beginning with:

```
f.seek(0)
```

Standard File Objects

Like many other languages, there are built-in file objects representing standard input, output, and error. These are in the sys module and are called stdin, stdout, and stderr. There are also immutable copies of these in __stdin__, __stdout__, and __stderr__. This is for IDLE and other tools in which the standard files have been changed.

You must import the sys module to use the special stdin, stdout, stderr I/O handles.

```
import sys
```

For finer control over input, use sys.stdin.read(). In order to implement the UNIX 'cat' program in Python, you could do something like this:

```
import sys
for line in sys.stdin:
    print line,
```

Also important is the sys.argv array. sys.argv is an array that contains the command-line arguments passed to the program.

```
python program.py hello there programmer!
```

This array can be indexed,and the arguments evaluated. In the above example, sys.argv[2] would contain the string "there", because the name of the program ("program.py") is stored in argv[0]. For more complicated command-line argument processing, see also(getopt module)

Output

The basic way to do output is the print statement.

```
print 'Hello, world'
```

This code ought to be obvious.

In order to print multiple things on the same line, use commas between them, like so:

```
print 'Hello,', 'World'
```

This will print out the following:

```
Hello, World
```

Note that although neither string contained a space, a space was added by the print statement because of the comma between the two objects. Arbitrary data types can be printed this way:

```
print 1,2,0xff,0777,(10+5j),-0.999,map,sys
```

This will print out:

```
1 2 255 511 (10+5j) -0.999 <built-in function map> <module 'sys' (built-in)>
```

Objects can be printed on the same line without needing to be on the same line if one puts a comma at the end of a print statement:

```
for i in range(10):
    print i,
```

will output:

```
0 1 2 3 4 5 6 7 8 9
```

In order to end this line, it may be necessary to add a print statement without any objects.

```
for i in range(10):
    print i,
print
for i in range(10,20):
    print i,
```

will output:

```
0 1 2 3 4 5 6 7 8 9
10 11 12 13 14 15 16 17 18 19
```

If the bare print statement were not present, the above output would look like:

```
0 1 2 3 4 5 6 7 8 9 10 11 12 13 14 15 16 17 18 19
```

printing without commas or newlines

If it is not desirable to add spaces between objects, but you want to run them all together on one line, there are several techniques for doing that.

concatenation

Concatenate the string representations of each object, then later print the whole thing at once.

```
print
str(1)+str(2)+str(0xff)+str(0777)+str(10+5j)+str(-0.999)+str(map)+str(sys)
```

will output:

```
12255511(10+5j)-0.999<built-in function map><module 'sys' (built-in)>
```

write

you can make a shorthand for *sys.stdout.write* and use that for output.

```
import sys
write = sys.stdout.write
write('20')
write('05\n')
```

will output:

```
2005
```

You may need sys.stdout.flush() to get that text on the screen quickly.

It is also possible to use similar syntax when writing to a file, instead of to standard output, like so:

```
print >> f, 'Hello, world'
```

This will print to any object that implements write(), which includes file objects.

| Previous: Exceptions | Index | Next: Modules |

Python Programming/Modules

| Previous: Input and output | Index | Next: Classes |

Modules are a simple way to structure a program. Mostly, there are modules in the standard library and there are other Python files, or directories containing Python files, in the current directory (each of which constitute a module). You can also instruct Python to search other directories for modules by placing their paths in the PYTHONPATH environment variable.

Importing a Module

Modules in Python are used by importing them. For example,

```
import math
```

This imports the math standard module. All of the functions in that module are namespaced by the module name, i.e.

```
import math
print math.sqrt(10)
```

This is often a nuisance, so other syntaxes are available to simplify this,

```
from string import whitespace
from math import *
from math import sin as SIN
from math import cos as COS
from ftplib import FTP as ftp_connection
print sqrt(10)
```

The first statement means whitespace is added to the current scope (but nothing else is). The second statement means that all the elements in the math namespace is added to the current scope.

Modules can be three different kinds of things:

- Python files
- Shared Objects (under Unix and Linux) with the .so suffix
- DLL's (under Windows) with the .pyd suffix
- directories

Modules are loaded in the order they're found, which is controlled by sys.path. The current directory is always on the path.

Directories should include a file in them called __init__.py, which should probably include the other files in the directory.

Creating a DLL that interfaces with Python is covered in another section.

Creating a Module

From a File

The easiest way to create a module by having a file called mymod.py either in a directory recognized by the PYTHONPATH variable or (even easier) in the same directory where you are working. If you have the following file mymod.py

```python
class Object1:
        def __init__(self):
                self.name = 'object 1'
```

you can already import this "module" and create instances of the object *Object1*.

```python
import mymod
myobject = mymod.Object1()
from mymod import *
myobject = Object1()
```

From a Directory

It is not feasible for larger projects to keep all classes in a single file. It is often easier to store all files in directories and load all files with one command. Each directory needs to have a __init__.py file which contains python commands that are executed upon loading the directory.

Suppose we have two more objects called Object2 and Object3 and we want to load all three objects with one command. We then create a directory called *mymod* and we store three files called *Object1.py*, *Object2.py* and *Object3.py* in it. These files would then contain one object per file but this not required (although it adds clarity). We would then write the following *__init__.py* file:

```python
from Object1 import *
from Object2 import *
from Object3 import *


__all__ = ["Object1", "Object2", "Object3"]
```

The first three commands tell python what to do when somebody loads the module. The last statement defining __all__ tells python what to do when somebody executes *from mymod import *.* Usually we want to use parts of a module in other parts of a module, e.g. we want to use Object1 in Object2. We can do this easily with an *from . import *.* command as the following file *Object2.py* shows:

```python
from . import *


class Object2:
        def __init__(self):
                self.name = 'object 2'
                self.otherObject = Object1()
```

We can now start python and import *mymod* as we have in the previous section.

External links

- Python Documentation [1]

Previous: Input and output	Index	Next: Classes

References

[1] http://docs.python.org/tutorial/modules.html

Python Programming/Classes

Previous: Modules	Index	Next: MetaClasses

Classes are a way of aggregating similar data and functions. A class is basically a scope inside which various code (especially function definitions) is executed, and the locals to this scope become *attributes* of the class, and of any objects constructed by this class. An object constructed by a class is called an *instance* of that class.

Defining a Class

To define a class, use the following format:

```
class ClassName:
    ...
    ...
```

The capitalization in this class definition is the convention, but is not required by the language.

Instance Construction

The class is a callable object that constructs an instance of the class when called. To construct an instance of a class, "call" the class object:

```
f = Foo()
```

This constructs an instance of class Foo and creates a reference to it in f.

Class Members

In order to access the member of an instance of a class, use the syntax <class instance>.<member>. It is also possible to access the members of the class definition with <class name>.<member>.

Methods

A method is a function within a class. The first argument (methods must always take at least one argument) is always the instance of the class on which the function is invoked. For example

```
>>> class Foo:
...     def setx(self, x):
...         self.x = x
...     def bar(self):
...         print self.x
```

If this code were executed, nothing would happen, at least until an instance of Foo were constructed, and then bar were called on that instance.

Invoking Methods

Calling a method is much like calling a function, but instead of passing the instance as the first parameter like the list of formal parameters suggests, use the function as an attribute of the instance.

```
>>> f.setx(5)
>>> f.bar()
```

This will output

```
5
```

It is possible to call the method on an arbitrary object, by using it as an attribute of the defining class instead of an instance of that class, like so:

```
>>> Foo.setx(f,5)
>>> Foo.bar(f)
```

This will have the same output.

Dynamic Class Structure

As shown by the method setx above, the members of a Python class can change during runtime, not just their values, unlike classes in languages like C or Java. We can even delete f.x after running the code above.

```
>>> del f.x
>>> f.bar()

Traceback (most recent call last):
  File "<stdin>", line 1, in ?
  File "<stdin>", line 5, in bar
AttributeError: Foo instance has no attribute 'x'
```

Another effect of this is that we can change the definition of the Foo class during program execution. In the code below, we create a member of the Foo class definition named y. If we then create a new instance of Foo, it will now have this new member.

```
>>> Foo.y = 10
>>> g = Foo()
>>> g.y
10
```

Viewing Class Dictionaries

At the heart of all this is a dictionary that can be accessed by "vars(ClassName)"

```
>>> vars(g)
{}
```

At first, this output makes no sense. We just saw that g had the member y, so why isn't it in the member dictionary? If you remember, though, we put y in the class definition, Foo, not g.

```
>>> vars(Foo)
{'y': 10, 'bar': <function bar at 0x4d6a3c>, '__module__': '__main__',
```

```
  'setx': <function setx at 0x4d6a04>, '__doc__': None}
```

And there we have all the members of the Foo class definition. When Python checks for g.member, it first checks g's vars dictionary for "member," then Foo. If we create a new member of g, it will be added to g's dictionary, but not Foo's.

```
>>> g.setx(5)
>>> vars(g)
{'x': 5}
```

Note that if we now assign a value to g.y, we are not assigning that value to Foo.y. Foo.y will still be 10, but g.y will now override Foo.y

```
>>> g.y = 9
>>> vars(g)
{'y': 9, 'x': 5}
>>> vars(Foo)
{'y': 10, 'bar': <function bar at 0x4d6a3c>, '__module__': '__main__',
 'setx': <function setx at 0x4d6a04>, '__doc__': None}
```

Sure enough, if we check the values:

```
>>> g.y
9
>>> Foo.y
10
```

Note that f.y will also be 10, as Python won't find 'y' in vars(f), so it will get the value of 'y' from vars(Foo).

Some may have also noticed that the methods in Foo appear in the class dictionary along with the x and y. If you remember from the section on lambda forms, we can treat functions just like variables. This means that we can assign methods to a class during runtime in the same way we assigned variables. If you do this, though, remember that if we call a method of a class instance, the first parameter passed to the method will always be the class instance itself.

Changing Class Dictionaries

We can also access the members dictionary of a class using the __dict__ member of the class.

```
>>> g.__dict__
{'y': 9, 'x': 5}
```

If we add, remove, or change key-value pairs from g.__dict__, this has the same effect as if we had made those changes to the members of g.

```
>>> g.__dict__['z'] = -4
>>> g.z
-4
```

New Style Classes

New style classes were introduced in python 2.2. A new-style class is a class that has a built-in as its base, most commonly object. At a low level, a major difference between old and new classes is their type. Old class instances were all of type instance. New style class instances will return the same thing as x.__class__ for their type. This puts user defined classes on a level playing field with built-ins. Old/Classic classes are slated to disappear in Python 3000. With this in mind all development should use new style classes. New Style classes also add constructs like properties and static methods familiar to Java programmers.

Old/Classic Class

```
>>> class ClassicFoo:
...     def __init__(self):
...         pass
```

New Style Class

```
>>> class NewStyleFoo(object):
...     def __init__(self):
...         pass
```

Properties

Properties are attributes with getter and setter methods.

```
>>> class SpamWithProperties(object):
...     def __init__(self):
...         self.__egg = "MyEgg"
...     def getEgg(self):
...         return self.__egg
...     def setEgg(self,egg):
...         self.__egg = egg
...     egg = property(getEgg,setEgg)

>>> sp = SpamWithProperties()
>>> sp.egg
'MyEgg'
>>> sp.egg = "Eggs With Spam"
>>> sp.egg
'Eggs With Spam'
>>>
```

Static Methods

Static methods in Python are just like their counterparts in C++ or Java. Static methods have no "self" argument and don't require you to instantiate the class before using them. They can be defined using staticmethod()

```
>>> class StaticSpam(object):
...     def StaticNoSpam():
...         print "You can't have have the spam, spam, eggs and spam
without any spam... that's disgusting"
...     NoSpam = staticmethod(StaticNoSpam)

>>> StaticSpam.NoSpam()
```

```
'You can't have have the spam, spam, eggs and spam without any spam...
that's disgusting'
```

They can also be defined using the function decorator @staticmethod.

```
>>> class StaticSpam(object):
...     @staticmethod
...     def StaticNoSpam():
...         print "You can't have have the spam, spam, eggs and spam
without any spam... that's disgusting"
```

Inheritance

Like all object oriented languages, Python provides for inheritance. Inheritance is a simple concept by which a class can extend the facilities of another class, or in Python's case, multiple other classes. Use the following format for this:

```
class ClassName(superclass1,superclass2,superclass3,...):
    ...
```

The subclass will then have all the members of its superclasses. If a method is defined in the subclass and in the superclass, the member in the subclass will override the one in the superclass. In order to use the method defined in the superclass, it is necessary to call the method as an attribute on the defining class, as in Foo.setx(f,5) above:

```
>>> class Foo:
...     def bar(self):
...         print "I'm doing Foo.bar()"
...     x = 10
...
>>> class Bar(Foo):
...     def bar(self):
...         print "I'm doing Bar.bar()"
...         Foo.bar(self)
...     y = 9
...
>>> g = Bar()
>>> Bar.bar(g)
I'm doing Bar.bar()
I'm doing Foo.bar()
>>> g.y
9
>>> g.x
10
```

Once again, we can see what's going on under the hood by looking at the class dictionaries.

```
>>> vars(g)
{}
>>> vars(Bar)
{'y': 9, '__module__': '__main__', 'bar': <function bar at 0x4d6a04>,
 '__doc__': None}
>>> vars(Foo)
```

```
{'x': 10, '__module__': '__main__', 'bar': <function bar at 0x4d6994>,
 '__doc__': None}
```

When we call g.x, it first looks in the vars(g) dictionary, as usual. Also as above, it checks vars(Bar) next, since g is an instance of Bar. However, thanks to inheritance, Python will check vars(Foo) if it doesn't find x in vars(Bar).

Special Methods

There are a number of methods which have reserved names which are used for special purposes like mimicking numerical or container operations, among other things. All of these names begin and end with two underscores. It is convention that methods beginning with a single underscore are 'private' to the scope they are introduced within.

Initialization and Deletion

__init__

One of these purposes is constructing an instance, and the special name for this is '__init__'. __init__() is called before an instance is returned (it is not necessary to return the instance manually). As an example,

```
class A:
    def __init__(self):
        print 'A.__init__()'
a = A()
```

outputs

```
A.__init__()
```

__init__() can take arguments, in which case it is necessary to pass arguments to the class in order to create an instance. For example,

```
class Foo:
    def __init__ (self, printme):
        print printme
foo = Foo('Hi!')
```

outputs

```
Hi!
```

Here is an example showing the difference between using __init__() and not using __init__():

```
class Foo:
    def __init__ (self, x):
        print x
foo = Foo('Hi!')
class Foo2:
    def setx(self, x):
        print x
f = Foo2()
Foo2.setx(f,'Hi!')
```

outputs

```
Hi!
Hi!
```

__del__

Similarly, '__del__' is called when an instance is destroyed; e.g. when it is no longer referenced.

Representation

__str__

Converting an object to a string, as with the print statement or with the str() conversion function, can be overridden by overriding __str__. Usually, __str__ returns a formatted version of the objects content. This will NOT usually be something that can be executed.

Function	Operator
__str__	str(A)
__repr__	repr(A)
__unicode__	unicode(x) (2.x only)

For example:

```
class Bar:
    def __init__ (self, iamthis):
        self.iamthis = iamthis
    def __str__ (self):
        return self.iamthis
bar = Bar('apple')
print bar
```

outputs

```
apple
```

__repr__

This function is much like __str__(). If __str__ is not present but this one is, this function's output is used instead for printing. __repr__ is used to return a representation of the object in string form. In general, it can be executed to get back the original object.

For example:

```
class Bar:
    def __init__ (self, iamthis):
        self.iamthis = iamthis
    def __repr__(self):
        return "Bar('%s')" % self.iamthis
bar = Bar('apple')
bar
```

outputs (note the difference: now is not necessary to put it inside a print)

```
Bar('apple')
```

Attributes

__setattr__

This is the function which is in charge of setting attributes of a class. It is provided with the name and value of the variables being assigned. Each class, of course, comes with a default __setattr__ which simply sets the value of the variable, but we can override it.

```
>>> class Unchangable:
...     def __setattr__(self, name, value):
...         print "Nice try"
...
>>> u = Unchangable()
>>> u.x = 9
Nice try
>>> u.x

Traceback (most recent call last):
  File "<stdin>", line 1, in ?
AttributeError: Unchangable instance has no attribute 'x'
```

Function	Indirect form	Direct Form
__getattr__	getattr(A, B)	A.B
__setattr__	setattr(A, B, C)	A.B = C
__delattr__	delattr(A, B)	del A.B

__getattr__

Similar to __setattr__, except this function is called when we try to access a class member, and the default simply returns the value.

```
>>> class HiddenMembers:
...     def __getattr__(self, name):
...         return "You don't get to see " + name
...
>>> h = HiddenMembers()
>>> h.anything
"You don't get to see anything"
```

__delattr__

This function is called to delete an attribute.

```
>>> class Permanent:
...     def __delattr__(self, name):
...         print name, "cannot be deleted"
...
>>> p = Permanent()
>>> p.x = 9
>>> del p.x
x cannot be deleted
>>> p.x
9
```

Operator Overloading

Operator overloading allows us to use the built-in Python syntax and operators to call functions which we define.

Binary Operators

If a class has the __add__ function, we can use the '+' operator to add instances of the class. This will call __add__ with the two instances of the class passed as parameters, and the return value will be the result of the addition.

```
>>> class FakeNumber:
...      n = 5
...      def __add__(A,B):
...          return A.n + B.n
...
>>> c = FakeNumber()
>>> d = FakeNumber()
>>> d.n = 7
>>> c + d
12
```

To override the augmented assignment operators, merely add 'i' in front of the normal binary operator, i.e. for '+=' use '__iadd__' instead of '__add__'. The function will be given one argument, which will be the object on the right side of the augmented assignment operator. The returned value of the function will then be assigned to the object on the left of the operator.

```
>>> c.__imul__ = lambda B: B.n - 6
>>> c *= d
>>> c
1
```

It is important to note that the augmented assignment operators will also use the normal operator functions if the augmented operator function hasn't been set directly. This will work as expected, with "__add__" being called for "+=" and so on.

```
>>> c = FakeNumber()
>>> c += d
>>> c
12
```

Function	Operator
__add__	A + B
__sub__	A - B
__mul__	A * B
__div__	A / B
__floordiv__	A // B
__mod__	A % B
__pow__	A ** B
__and__	A & B
__or__	A | B
__xor__	A ^ B
__eq__	A == B
__ne__	A != B
__gt__	A > B
__lt__	A < B
__ge__	A >= B
__le__	A <= B
__lshift__	A << B
__rshift__	A >> B
__contains__	A in B A not in B

Unary Operators

Unary operators will be passed simply the instance of the class that they are called on.

```
>>> FakeNumber.__neg__ = lambda A : A.n + 6
>>> -d
13
```

Function	Operator
__pos__	+A
__neg__	-A
__inv__	~A
__abs__	abs(A)
__len__	len(A)

Item Operators

It is also possible in Python to override the indexing and slicing operators. This allows us to use the class[i] and class[a:b] syntax on our own objects.

The simplest form of item operator is __getitem__. This takes as a parameter the instance of the class, then the value of the index.

Function	Operator
__getitem__	C[i]
__setitem__	C[i] = v
__delitem__	del C[i]
__getslice__	C[s:e]
__setslice__	C[s:e] = v
__delslice__	del C[s:e]

```
>>> class FakeList:
...        def __getitem__(self,index):
...             return index * 2
...
>>> f = FakeList()
>>> f['a']
'aa'
```

We can also define a function for the syntax associated with assigning a value to an item. The parameters for this function include the value being assigned, in addition to the parameters from __getitem__

```
>>> class FakeList:
...        def __setitem__(self,index,value):
...             self.string = index + " is now " + value
...
>>> f = FakeList()
>>> f['a'] = 'gone'
>>> f.string
'a is now gone'
```

We can do the same thing with slices. Once again, each syntax has a different parameter list associated with it.

```
>>> class FakeList:
...        def __getslice__(self,start,end):
...             return str(start) + " to " + str(end)
...
>>> f = FakeList()
>>> f[1:4]
'1 to 4'
```

Keep in mind that one or both of the start and end parameters can be blank in slice syntax. Here, Python has default value for both the start and the end, as show below.

```
>> f[:]
'0 to 2147483647'
```

Note that the default value for the end of the slice shown here is simply the largest possible signed integer on a 32-bit system, and may vary depending on your system and C compiler.

* __setslice__ has the parameters (self,start,end,value)

We also have operators for deleting items and slices.

* __delitem__ has the parameters (self,index)
* __delslice__ has the parameters (self,start,end)

Note that these are the same as __getitem__ and __getslice__.

Other Overrides

Function	Operator
__cmp__	cmp(x, y)
__hash__	hash(x)
__nonzero__	bool(x)
__call__	f(x)
__iter__	iter(x)
__reversed__	reversed(x) (2.6+)
__divmod__	divmod(x, y)
__int__	int(x)
__long__	long(x)
__float__	float(x)
__complex__	complex(x)
__hex__	hex(x)
__oct__	oct(x)
__index__	
__copy__	copy.copy(x)
__deepcopy__	copy.deepcopy(x)
__sizeof__	sys.getsizeof(x) (2.6+)
__trunc__	math.trunc(x) (2.6+)
__format__	format(x, ...) (2.6+)

Programming Practices

The flexibility of python classes means that classes can adopt a varied set of behaviors. For the sake of understandability, however, it's best to use many of Python's tools sparingly. Try to declare all methods in the class definition, and always use the <class>.<member> syntax instead of __dict__ whenever possible. Look at classes in C++ and Java to see what most programmers will expect from a class.

Encapsulation

Since all python members of a python class are accessible by functions/methods outside the class, there is no way to enforce encapsulation short of overriding __getattr__, __setattr__ and __delattr__. General practice, however, is for the creator of a class or module to simply trust that users will use only the intended interface and avoid limiting access to the workings of the module for the sake of users who do need to access it. When using parts of a class or module other than the intended interface, keep in mind that the those parts may change in later versions of the module, and you may even cause errors or undefined behaviors in the module.

Doc Strings

When defining a class, it is convention to document the class using a string literal at the start of the class definition. This string will then be placed in the __doc__ attribute of the class definition.

```
>>> class Documented:
...        """This is a docstring"""
...        def explode(self):
...            """
...            This method is documented, too! The coder is really serious
 about
...            making this class usable by others who don't know the code
as well
...            as he does.
...
...            """
...            print "boom"
>>> d = Documented()
>>> d.__doc__
'This is a docstring'
```

Docstrings are a very useful way to document your code. Even if you never write a single piece of separate documentation (and let's admit it, doing so is the lowest priority for many coders), including informative docstrings in your classes will go a long way toward making them usable.

Several tools exist for turning the docstrings in Python code into readable API documentation, *e.g.*, EpyDoc [1].

Don't just stop at documenting the class definition, either. Each method in the class should have its own docstring as well. Note that the docstring for the method *explode* in the example class *Documented* above has a fairly lengthy docstring that spans several lines. Its formatting is in accordance with the style suggestions of Python's creator, Guido van Rossum.

Adding methods at runtime

To a class

It is fairly easy to add methods to a class at runtime. Lets assume that we have a class called *Spam* and a function cook. We want to be able to use the function cook on all instances of the class Spam:

```
class Spam:
  def __init__(self):
    self.myeggs = 5


def cook(self):
  print "cooking %s eggs" % self.myeggs


Spam.cook = cook      #add the function to the class Spam
eggs = Spam()         #NOW create a new instance of Spam
eggs.cook()           #and we are ready to cook!
```

This will output

```
cooking 5 eggs
```

To an instance of a class

It is a bit more tricky to add methods to an instance of a class that has already been created. Lets assume again that we have a class called *Spam* and we have already created eggs. But then we notice that we wanted to cook those eggs, but we do not want to create a new instance but rather use the already created one:

```python
class Spam:
  def __init__(self):
    self.myeggs = 5

eggs = Spam()

def cook(self):
  print "cooking %s eggs" % self.myeggs

import types
f = types.MethodType(cook, eggs, Spam)
eggs.cook = f

eggs.cook()
```

Now we can cook our eggs and the last statement will output:

```
cooking 5 eggs
```

Using a function

We can also write a function that will make the process of adding methods to an instance of a class easier.

```python
def attach_method(fxn, instance, myclass):
  f = types.MethodType(fxn, instance, myclass)
  setattr(instance, fxn.__name__, f)
```

All we now need to do is call the attach_method with the arguments of the function we want to attach, the instance we want to attach it to and the class the instance is derived from. Thus our function call might look like this:

```
attach_method(cook, eggs, Spam)
```

Note that in the function add_method we cannot write `instance.fxn = f` since this would add a function called fxn to the instance.

Previous: Modules	Index	Next: MetaClasses

References

[1] http://epydoc.sourceforge.net/using.html

Python Programming/MetaClasses

Previous: Classes	Index	Next: Standard Library

In python, classes are themselves objects. Just as other objects are instances of a particular class, classes themselves are instances of a metaclass.

Class Factories

The simplest use of python metaclasses is a class factory. This concept makes use of the fact that class definitions in python are first-class objects. Such a function can create or modify a class definition, using the same syntax one would normally use in declaring a class definition. Once again, it is useful to use the model of classes as dictionaries. First, let's look at a basic class factory:

```
>>> def StringContainer():
...     # define a class
...     class String:
...         content_string = ""
...         def len(self):
...             return len(self.content_string)
...     # return the class definition
...     return String
...
>>> # create the class definition
... container_class = StringContainer()
>>>
>>> # create an instance of the class
... wrapped_string = container_class()
>>>
>>> # take it for a test drive
... wrapped_string.content_string = 'emu emissary'
>>> wrapped_string.len()
12
```

Of course, just like any other data in python, class definitions can also be modified. Any modifications to attributes in a class definition will be seen in any instances of that definition, so long as that instance hasn't overridden the attribute that you're modifying.

```
>>> def DeAbbreviate(sequence_container):
...     setattr(sequence_container, 'length', sequence_container.len)
...     delattr(sequence_container, 'len')
...
>>> DeAbbreviate(container_class)
>>> wrapped_string.length()
12
>>> wrapped_string.len()
 Traceback (most recent call last):
   File "<stdin>", line 1, in ?
```

```
AttributeError: String instance has no attribute 'len'
```

You can also delete class definitions, but that will not affect instances of the class.

```
>>> del container_class
>>> wrapped_string2 = container_class()
Traceback (most recent call last):
  File "<stdin>", line 1, in ?
NameError: name 'container_class' is not defined
>>> wrapped_string.length()
12
```

The type Metaclass

The metaclass for all standard python types is the "type" object.

```
>>> type(object)
<type 'type'>
>>> type(int)
<type 'type'>
>>> type(list)
<type 'type'>
```

Just like list, int and object, "type" is itself a normal python object, and is itself an instance of a class. In this case, it is in fact an instance of itself.

```
>>> type(type)
<type 'type'>
```

It can be instantiated to create new class objects similarly to the class factory example above by passing the name of the new class, the base classes to inherit from, and a dictionary defining the namespace to use.

For instance, the code:

```
>>> class MyClass(BaseClass):
...     attribute = 42
```

Could also be written as:

```
>>> MyClass = type("MyClass", (BaseClass,), {'attribute' : 42})
```

Metaclasses

It is possible to create a class with a different metaclass than type by setting its __metaclass__ attribute when defining. When this is done, the class, and its subclass will be created using your custom metaclass. For example

```
class CustomMetaclass(type):
    def __init__(cls, name, bases, dct):
        print "Creating class %s using CustomMetaclass" % name
        super(CustomMetaclass, cls).__init__(name, bases, dct)

class BaseClass(object):
    __metaclass__ = CustomMetaclass

class Subclass1(BaseClass):
```

```
    pass
```

This will print

```
Creating class BaseClass using CustomMetaclass
Creating class Subclass1 using CustomMetaclass
```

By creating a custom metaclass in this way, it is possible to change how the class is constructed. This allows you to add or remove attributes and methods, register creation of classes and subclasses creation and various other manipulations when the class is created.

More resources

- Wikipedia article on Aspect Oriented Programming
- Unifying types and classes in Python 2.2 [1]
- O'Reilly Article on Python Metaclasses [2]

[Incomplete] (see Putting Metaclasses to Work, Ira R. Forman, Scott H. Danforth?)

Previous: Classes	Index	Next: Standard Library

References

[1] http://www.python.org/2.2/descrintro.html
[2] http://www.onlamp.com/pub/a/python/2003/04/17/metaclasses.html

Modules

Python Programming/Standard Library

| Previous: MetaClasses | Index | Next: Regular Expression |

The Python Standard Library is a collection of script modules accessible to a Python program to simplify the programming process and removing the need to rewrite commonly used commands. They can be used by 'calling' them at the beginning of a script.

| Previous: MetaClasses | Index | Next: Regular Expression |

Python Programming/Regular Expression

| Previous: Standard Library | Index | Next: XML Tools |

Python includes a module for working with regular expressions on strings. For more information about writing regular expressions and syntax not specific to Python, see the regular expressions wikibook. Python's regular expression syntax is similar to Perl's

To start using regular expressions in your Python scripts, just import the "re" module:

```
import re
```

Pattern objects

If you're going to be using the same regexp more than once in a program, or if you just want to keep the regexps separated somehow, you should create a pattern object, and refer to it later when searching/replacing.

To create a pattern object, use the compile function.

```
import re
foo = re.compile(r'foo(.{,5})bar', re.I+re.S)
```

The first argument is the pattern, which matches the string "foo", followed by up to 5 of any character, then the string "bar", storing the middle characters to a group, which will be discussed later. The second, optional, argument is the flag or flags to modify the regexp's behavior. The flags themselves are simply variables referring to an integer used by the regular expression engine. In other languages, these would be constants, but Python does not have constants. Some of the regular expression functions do not support adding flags as a parameter when defining the pattern directly in the function, if you need any of the flags, it is best to use the compile function to create a pattern object.

The r preceding the expression string indicates that it should be treated as a raw string. This should normally be used when writing regexps, so that backslashes are interpreted literally rather than having to be escaped.

The different flags are:

Abbreviation	Full name	Description
re.I	re.IGNORECASE	Makes the regexp case-insensitive
re.L	re.LOCALE	Makes the behavior of some special sequences (\w, \W, \b, \B, \s, \S) dependant on the current locale
re.M	re.MULTILINE	Makes the ^ and $ characters match at the beginning and end of each line, rather than just the beginning and end of the string
re.S	re.DOTALL	Makes the . character match every character *including* newlines.
re.U	re.UNICODE	Makes \w, \W, \b, \B, \d, \D, \s, \S dependent on Unicode character properties
re.X	re.VERBOSE	Ignores whitespace except when in a character class or preceded by an non-escaped backslash, and ignores # (except when in a character class or preceded by an non-escaped backslash) and everything after it to the end of a line, so it can be used as a comment. This allows for cleaner-looking regexps.

Matching and searching

One of the most common uses for regular expressions is extracting a part of a string or testing for the existence of a pattern in a string. Python offers several functions to do this.

The match and search functions do mostly the same thing, except that the match function will only return a result if the pattern matches at the beginning of the string being searched, while search will find a match anywhere in the string.

```
>>> import re
>>> foo = re.compile(r'foo(.{,5})bar', re.I+re.S)
>>> st1 = 'Foo, Bar, Baz'
>>> st2 = '2. foo is bar'
>>> search1 = foo.search(st1)
>>> search2 = foo.search(st2)
>>> match1 = foo.match(st1)
>>> match2 = foo.match(st2)
```

In this example, match2 will be None, because the string st2 does not start with the given pattern. The other 3 results will be Match objects (see below).

You can also match and search without compiling a regexp:

```
>>> search3 = re.search('oo.*ba', st1, re.I)
```

Here we use the search function of the re module, rather than of the pattern object. For most cases, its best to compile the expression first. Not all of the re module functions support the flags argument and if the expression is used more than once, compiling first is more efficient and leads to cleaner looking code.

The compiled pattern object functions also have parameters for starting and ending the search, to search in a substring of the given string. In the first example in this section, match2 returns no result because the pattern does not start at the beginning of the string, but if we do:

```
>>> match3 = foo.match(st2, 3)
```

it works, because we tell it to start searching at character number 3 in the string.

What if we want to search for multiple instances of the pattern? Then we have two options. We can use the start and end position parameters of the search and match function in a loop, getting the position to start at from the previous match object (see below) or we can use the findall and finditer functions. The findall function returns a list of matching strings, useful for simple searching. For anything slightly complex, the finditer function should be used.

This returns an iterator object, that when used in a loop, yields Match objects. For example:

```
>>> str3 = 'foo, Bar Foo. BAR FoO: bar'
>>> foo.findall(str3)
[', ', '. ', ': ']
>>> for match in foo.finditer(str3):
...         match.group(1)
...
', '
'. '
': '
```

If you're going to be iterating over the results of the search, using the finditer function is almost always a better choice.

Match objects

Match objects are returned by the search and match functions, and include information about the pattern match.

The group function returns a string corresponding to a capture group (part of a regexp wrapped in ()) of the expression, or if no group number is given, the entire match. Using the search1 variable we defined above:

```
>>> search1.group()
'Foo, Bar'
>>> search1.group(1)
', '
```

 Capture groups can also be given string names using a special syntax and referred to by matchobj.group('name'). For simple expressions this is unnecessary, but for more complex expressions it can be very useful.

You can also get the position of a match or a group in a string, using the start and end functions:

```
>>> search1.start()
0
>>> search1.end()
8
>>> search1.start(1)
3
>>> search1.end(1)
5
```

This returns the start and end locations of the entire match, and the start and end of the first (and in this case only) capture group, respectively.

Replacing

Another use for regular expressions is replacing text in a string. To do this in Python, use the sub function.

sub takes up to 3 arguments: The text to replace with, the text to replace in, and, optionally, the maximum number of substitutions to make. Unlike the matching and searching functions, sub returns a string, consisting of the given text with the substitution(s) made.

```
>>> import re
>>> mystring = 'This string has a q in it'
>>> pattern = re.compile(r'(a[n]? )(\w) ')
>>> newstring = pattern.sub(r"\1'\2' ", mystring)
>>> newstring
"This string has a 'q' in it"
```

This takes any single alphanumeric character (\w in regular expression syntax) preceded by "a" or "an" and wraps in in single quotes. The \1 and \2 in the replacement string are backreferences to the 2 capture groups in the expression; these would be group(1) and group(2) on a Match object from a search.

The subn function is similar to sub, except it returns a tuple, consisting of the result string and the number of replacements made. Using the string and expression from before:

```
>>> subresult = pattern.subn(r"\1'\2' ", mystring)
>>> subresult
("This string has a 'q' in it", 1)
```

Other functions

The re module has a few other functions in addition to those discussed above.

The split function splits a string based on a given regular expression:

```
>>> import re
>>> mystring = '1. First part 2. Second part 3. Third part'
>>> re.split(r'\d\.', mystring)
['', ' First part ', ' Second part ', ' Third part']
```

The escape function escapes all non-alphanumeric characters in a string. This is useful if you need to take an unknown string that may contain regexp metacharacters like (and . and create a regular expression from it.

```
>>> re.escape(r'This text (and this) must be escaped with a "\" to use in
a regexp.')
'This\\ text\\ \\(and\\ this\\)\\ must\\ be\\ escaped\\ with\\ a\\
\\"\\\\\\\\"\\ to\\ use\\ in\\ a\\ regexp\\.'
```

External links

- Python re documentation [1] - Full documentation for the re module, including pattern objects and match objects

Previous: Standard Library	Index	Next: XML Tools

References

[1] http://docs.python.org/library/re.html

Python Programming/XML Tools

Previous: Regular Expression	Index	Next: Email

Introduction

Python includes several modules for manipulating xml.

xml.sax.handler

Python Doc [1]

```python
import xml.sax.handler as saxhandler
import xml.sax as saxparser

class MyReport:
    def __init__(self):
        self.Y = 1


class MyCH(saxhandler.ContentHandler):
    def __init__(self, report):
        self.X = 1
        self.report = report

    def startDocument(self):
        print 'startDocument'

    def startElement(self, name, attrs):
        print 'Element:', name

report = MyReport()              #for future use
ch = MyCH(report)


xml = """\
<collection>
  <comic title=\"Sandman\" number='62'>
```

```
        <writer>Neil Gaiman</writer>
        <penciller pages='1-9,18-24'>Glyn Dillon</penciller>
        <penciller pages="10-17">Charles Vess</penciller>
    </comic>
</collection>
"""

print xml

saxparser.parseString(xml, ch)
```

xml.dom.minidom

An example of doing RSS feed parsing with DOM

```
from xml.dom import minidom as dom
import urllib2

def fetchPage(url):
    a = urllib2.urlopen(url)
    return ''.join(a.readlines())

def extract(page):
    a = dom.parseString(page)
    item = a.getElementsByTagName('item')
    for i in item:
        if i.hasChildNodes() == True:
            t = i.getElementsByTagName('title')[0].firstChild.wholeText
            l = i.getElementsByTagName('link')[0].firstChild.wholeText
            d =
i.getElementsByTagName('description')[0].firstChild.wholeText
            print t, l, d

if __name__=='__main__':
    page = fetchPage("http://rss.slashdot.org/Slashdot/slashdot")
    extract(page)
```

XML document provided by pyxml documentation [2].

Previous: Regular Expression	Index	Next: Email

References

[1] http://docs.python.org/lib/module-xml.sax.handler.html
[2] http://pyxml.sourceforge.net/topics/howto/node12.html

Python Programming/Email

Previous: XML Tools	Index	Next: Threading

Python includes several modules in the standard library for working with emails and email servers.

Sending mail

Sending mail is done with Python's smtplib using an SMTP (Simple Mail Transfer Protocol) server. Actual usage varies depending on complexity of the email and settings of the email server, the instructions here are based on sending email through Google's Gmail.

The first step is to create an SMTP object, each object is used for connection with one server.

```
import smtplib
server = smtplib.SMTP('smtp.gmail.com', 587)
```

The first argument is the server's hostname, the second is the port. The port used varies depending on the server.

Next, we need to do a few steps to set up the proper connection for sending mail.

```
server.ehlo()
server.starttls()
server.ehlo()
```

These steps may not be necessary depending on the server you connect to. ehlo() is used for ESMTP servers, for non-ESMTP servers, use helo() instead. See Wikipedia's article about the SMTP protocol for more information about this. The starttls() function starts Transport Layer Security mode, which is required by Gmail. Other mail systems may not use this, or it may not be available.

Next, log in to the server:

```
server.login("youremailusername", "password")
```

Then, send the mail:

```
msg = "\nHello!" # The /n separates the message from the headers (which
 we ignore for this example)
server.sendmail("you@gmail.com", "target@example.com", msg)
```

Note that this is a rather crude example, it doesn't include a subject, or any other headers. For that, one should use the email package.

The email package

Python's email package contains many classes and functions for composing and parsing email messages, this section only covers a small subset useful for sending emails.

We start by only importing only the classes we need, this also saves us from having to use the full module name later.

```
from email.MIMEMultipart import MIMEMultipart
from email.MIMEText import MIMEText
```

Then we compose some of the basic message headers:

```
fromaddr = "you@gmail.com"
toaddr = "target@example.com"
msg = MIMEMultipart()
msg['From'] = fromaddr
msg['To'] = toaddr
msg['Subject'] = "Python email"
```

Next, we attach the body of the email to the MIME message:

```
body = "Python test mail"
msg.attach(MIMEText(body, 'plain'))
```

For sending the mail, we have to convert the object to a string, and then use the same prodecure as above to send using the SMTP server..

```
import smtplib
server = smtplib.SMTP('smtp.gmail.com', 587)
server.ehlo()
server.starttls()
server.ehlo()
server.login("youremailusername", "password")
text = msg.as_string()
server.sendmail(fromaddr, toaddr, text)
```

If we look at the text, we can see it has added all the necessary headers and structure necessary for a MIME formatted email. See MIME for more details on the standard:

The full text of our example message
| ```
>>> print text
Content-Type: multipart/mixed; boundary="===============1893313573=="
MIME-Version: 1.0
From: you@gmail.com
To: target@example.com
Subject: Python email

--===============1893313573==
Content-Type: text/plain; charset="us-ascii"
MIME-Version: 1.0
Content-Transfer-Encoding: 7bit

Python test mail
--===============1893313573==--
``` |
```

Previous: XML Tools	Index	Next: Threading

Python Programming/Threading

Previous: Email	Index	Next: Sockets

Threading in python is used to run multiple threads (tasks, function calls) at the same time. Note that this does not mean, that they are executed on different CPUs. Python threads will NOT make your program faster if it already uses 100 % CPU time, probably you then want to look into parallel programming. If you are interested in parallel progamming with python, please see here [1].

Python threads are used in cases where the execution of a task involves some waiting. One example would be interaction with a service hosted on another computer, such as a webserver. Threading allows python to execute other code while waiting; this is easily simulated with the sleep function.

Examples

A Minimal Example with Function Call

Make a thread that prints numbers from 1-10, waits for 1 sec between:

```
import thread, time

def loop1_10():
    for i in range(1,10):
        time.sleep(1)
        print i

thread.start_new_thread(loop1_10, ())
```

A Minimal Example with Object

```
#!/usr/bin/env python
import threading
import time

class MyThread(threading.Thread):
    def run(self):
        print "%s started!" % self.getName()
        time.sleep(1)
        print "%s finished!" % self.getName()

if __name__ == '__main__':
    for x in range(4):
        mythread = MyThread(name = "Thread-%d" % (x + 1))
        mythread.start()
```

```
            time.sleep(.2)
```

This should output:

```
Thread-1 started!
Thread-2 started!
Thread-3 started!
Thread-4 started!
Thread-1 finished!
Thread-2 finished!
Thread-3 finished!
Thread-4 finished!
```

Note: this example appears to crash IDLE in Windows XP (seems to work in IDLE 1.2.4 in Windows XP though)

There seems to be a problem with this, if you replace Sleep(1) with (2) ,and change range (4) to range(10). Thread -2 finished is the first line before its even started. in WING IDE, Netbeans, eclipse is fine.

Previous: Email	Index	Next: Sockets

References

[1] http://wiki.python.org/moin/ParallelProcessing

Python Programming/Sockets

Previous: Threading	Index	Next: GUI Programming

HTTP Client

Make a very simple HTTP client

```python
import socket
s = socket.socket()
s.connect(('localhost', 80))
s.send('GET / HTTP/1.1\nHost:localhost\n\n')
s.recv(40000) # receive 40000 bytes
```

NTP/Sockets

Connecting to and reading an NTP time server, returning the time as follows

```
ntpps       picoseconds portion of time
ntps        seconds portion of time
ntpms       milliseconds portion of time
ntpt        64-bit ntp time, seconds in upper 32-bits, picoseconds in lower 32-bits
```

```python
import socket
import sys
```

```python
import time

BLOCKING = 1               # 0 = non blocking, 1 = blocking
NONBLOCKING = 0            # 0 = non blocking, 1 = blocking
TIME1970           = 2208988800L       # Thanks to F.Lundh
NTPPORT            = 123
MAXLEN             = 1024
NTPSERVER          = ('time.apple.com')
SKTRDRETRYCOUNT       = 2
SKTRDRETRYDLY         = 0.01


#*****************************************************
## opensocket(servername, port, blocking) \n
# opens a socket at ip address "servername"
# \arg servername = ip address to open a socket to
# \arg port = port number to use
# ntp uses dgram sockets instead of stream
def opensocket(ipaddr, port, mode):
    # create the socket
    skt = socket.socket(socket.AF_INET, socket.SOCK_DGRAM)

    # open the socket
    try:
        skt.connect((ipaddr, port))
    except socket.error, e:
        print "Failed to connect to server %s %d %d" % (ipaddr, port,
mode)
        print "Error %s" % (e.args[0])
        print "Goodbye..."
        sys.exit()

    # set the blocking mode (0=nonblocking, 1=blocking)
    try:
        skt.setblocking(mode)
    except socket.error, e:
        print "Failed to set socket blocking mode for %s %d %d"
%(ipaddr, port, mode)
        print "Error %s" % (e.args[0])
        print "Goodbye..."
        sys.exit()

    return(skt)


#*****************************************************
##
# we should get 12 long words back in network order \n
# the 10th word is the transmit time (seconds since UT 1900-Jan-01 \n
```

```
#  I = unsigned long integer \n
#  ! = network (big endian) ordering
#  \arg \c \b ntpsocket, the socket handle to connect to
#  \arg \c \b msg, the message to send to the ntp server
def getntptime(ntpsocket, msg, servername):
    ntpsocket.send(msg)

    rtrycnt = 0
    data = 0
    while (data == 0) & (rtrycnt < SKTRDRETRYCOUNT):
        try:
            data = ntpsocket.recv(MAXLEN)
        except socket.error, e:
            rtrycnt += 1
            print "Error reading non-blocking socket, retries = %s,
server = %s" %(rtrycnt, servername)
            time.sleep(SKTRDRETRYDLY)        # don't retry too often

    # check and see if we got valid data back
    if data:
        ntps = unpack('!12I', data)[10]
        ntpps = unpack('!12I', data)[11]
        if ntps == 0:
            print "Error: NTP, invalid response, goodbye..."
            sys.exit()
    else:
        print "Error: NTP, no data returned, goodbye..."
        sys.exit()

    ntpms = ntpps/5000000L                   # 1ms/200ps, we want ms
    ntpt = (ntps << 32) + ntpps
    return (ntpsocket, ntps, ntpps, ntpms, ntpt)
```

Previous: Threading	Index	Next: GUI Programming

Python Programming/GUI Programming

| Previous: Sockets | Index | Next: WSGI web programming |

There are various GUI toolkits to start with.

Tkinter

Tkinter, a Python wrapper for Tcl/Tk, comes bundled with Python (at least on Win32 platform though it can be installed on Unix/Linux and Mac machines) and provides a cross-platform GUI. It is a relatively simple to learn yet powerful toolkit that provides what appears to be a modest set of widgets. However, because the Tkinter widgets are extensible, many compound widgets can be created rather easily (i.e. combo-box, scrolled panes). Because of its maturity and extensive documentation Tkinter has been designated as the de facto GUI for Python.

To create a very simple Tkinter window frame one only needs the following lines of code:

```
import Tkinter


root = Tkinter.Tk()
root.mainloop()
```

From an object-oriented perspective one can do the following:

```
import Tkinter


class App:
    def __init__(self, master):
        button = Tkinter.Button(master, text="I'm a Button.")
        button.pack()


if __name__ == '__main__':
    root = Tkinter.Tk()
    app = App(root)
    root.mainloop()
```

To learn more about Tkinter visit the following links:

- http://www.astro.washington.edu/owen/TkinterSummary.html <- A summary
- http://infohost.nmt.edu/tcc/help/lang/python/tkinter.html <- A tutorial
- http://www.pythonware.com/library/tkinter/introduction/ <- A reference

PyGTK

See also book PyGTK For GUI Programming

PyGTK [1] provides a convenient wrapper for the GTK+ [2] library for use in Python programs, taking care of many of the boring details such as managing memory and type casting. The bare GTK+ toolkit runs on Linux, Windows, and Mac OS X (port in progress), but the more extensive features — when combined with PyORBit and gnome-python — require a GNOME [3] install, and can be used to write full featured GNOME applications.

Home Page [1]

PyQt

PyQt is a wrapper around the cross-platform Qt C++ toolkit [4]. It has many widgets and support classes [5] supporting SQL, OpenGL, SVG, XML, and advanced graphics capabilities. A PyQt hello world example:

```python
from PyQt4.QtCore import *
from PyQt4.QtGui import *


class App(QApplication):
    def __init__(self, argv):
        super(App, self).__init__(argv)
        self.msg = QLabel("Hello, World!")
        self.msg.show()


if __name__ == "__main__":
    import sys
    app = App(sys.argv)
    sys.exit(app.exec_)
```

PyQt [6] is a set of bindings for the cross-platform Qt application framework. PyQt v4 supports Qt4 and PyQt v3 supports Qt3 and earlier.

wxPython

Bindings for the cross platform toolkit wxWidgets [7]. WxWidgets is available on Windows, Macintosh, and Unix/Linux.

```python
import wx


class test(wx.App):
    def __init__(self):
        wx.App.__init__(self, redirect=False)

    def OnInit(self):
        frame = wx.Frame(None, -1,
                         "Test",
                         pos=(50,50), size=(100,40),
                         style=wx.DEFAULT_FRAME_STYLE)
        button = wx.Button(frame, -1, "Hello World!", (20, 20))
        self.frame = frame
        self.frame.Show()
        return True


if __name__ == '__main__':
    app = test()
    app.MainLoop()
```

- wxPython [8]

Dabo

Dabo is a full 3-tier application framework. Its UI layer wraps wxPython, and greatly simplifies the syntax.

```python
import dabo
dabo.ui.loadUI("wx")

class TestForm(dabo.ui.dForm):
    def afterInit(self):
        self.Caption = "Test"
        self.Position = (50, 50)
        self.Size = (100, 40)
        self.btn = dabo.ui.dButton(self, Caption="Hello World",
            OnHit=self.onButtonClick)
        self.Sizer.append(self.btn, halign="center", border=20)

    def onButtonClick(self, evt):
        dabo.ui.info("Hello World!")

if __name__ == '__main__':
    app = dabo.ui.dApp()
    app.MainFormClass = TestForm
    app.start()
```

- Dabo [9]

pyFltk

pyFltk [10] is a Python wrapper for the FLTK [11], a lightweight cross-platform GUI toolkit. It is very simple to learn and allows for compact user interfaces.

The "Hello World" example in pyFltk looks like:

```python
from fltk import *

window = Fl_Window(100, 100, 200, 90)
button = Fl_Button(9,20,180,50)
button.label("Hello World")
window.end()
window.show()
Fl.run()
```

Other Toolkits

- PyKDE [12] - Part of the kdebindings package, it provides a python wrapper for the KDE libraries.
- PyXPCOM [13] provides a wrapper around the Mozilla XPCOM [14] component architecture, thereby enabling the use of standalone XUL [15] applications in Python. The XUL toolkit has traditionally been wrapped up in various other parts of XPCOM, but with the advent of libxul and XULRunner [16] this should become more feasible.

Previous: Sockets	Index	Next: WSGI web programming

References

[1] http://www.pygtk.org/
[2] http://www.gtk.org
[3] http://www.gnome.org
[4] http://www.trolltech.com/products/qt
[5] http://www.riverbankcomputing.com/Docs/PyQt4/html/classes.html
[6] http://www.riverbankcomputing.co.uk/pyqt/
[7] http://www.wxwidgets.org/
[8] http://wxpython.org/
[9] http://dabodev.com/
[10] http://pyfltk.sourceforge.net/
[11] http://www.fltk.org/
[12] http://www.riverbankcomputing.co.uk/pykde/index.php
[13] http://developer.mozilla.org/en/docs/PyXPCOM
[14] http://developer.mozilla.org/en/docs/XPCOM
[15] http://developer.mozilla.org/en/docs/XUL
[16] http://developer.mozilla.org/en/docs/XULRunner

Python Programming/WSGI web programming

Previous: GUI Programming	Index	Next: Web Page Harvesting

WSGI Web Programming

External Resources

http://docs.python.org/library/wsgiref.html

Previous: GUI Programming	Index	Next: Web Page Harvesting

Python Programming/Web Page Harvesting

Previous: WSGI web programming	Index	Next: Database Programming

Previous: WSGI web programming	Index	Next: Database Programming

Python Programming/Database Programming

Previous: Web Page Harvesting	Index	Next: Game Programming in Python

Generic Database Connectivity using ODBC

The Open Database Connectivity (ODBC) API standard allows transparent connections with any database that supports the interface. This includes most popular databases, such as PostgreSQL or Microsoft Access. The strengths of using this interface is that a Python script or module can be used on different databases by only modifying the connection string.

There are three ODBC modules for Python:

1. **PythonWin ODBC Module**: provided by Mark Hammond with the PythonWin [1] package for Microsoft Windows (only). This is a minimal implementation of ODBC, and conforms to Version 1.0 of the Python Database API. Although it is stable, it will likely not be developed any further.[2]
2. **mxODBC**: a commercial Python package (http://www.egenix.com/products/python/mxODBC/), which features handling of DateTime objects and prepared statements (using parameters).
3. **pyodbc**: an open-source Python package (http://code.google.com/p/pyodbc), which uses only native Python data-types and uses prepared statements for increased performance. The present version supports the Python Database API Specification v2.0.[3]

pyodbc

An example using the pyodbc Python package with a Microsoft Access file (although this database connection could just as easily be a MySQL database):

```python
import pyodbc

DBfile = '/data/MSAccess/Music_Library.mdb'
conn = pyodbc.connect('DRIVER={Microsoft Access Driver
(*.mdb)};DBQ='+DBfile)
cursor = conn.cursor()

SQL = 'SELECT Artist, AlbumName FROM RecordCollection ORDER BY Year;'
for row in cursor.execute(SQL): # cursors are iterable
    print row.Artist, row.AlbumName

cursor.close()
conn.close()
```

Many more features and examples are provided on the pyodbc website.

Postgres connection in Python

```
import psycopg2
conn = psycopg2.connect("dbname=test")
cursor = conn.cursor()
cursor.execute("select * from test");
for i in cursor.next():
    print i
conn.close()
```

SQLAlchemy in Action

SQLAlchemy has become the favorite choice for many large Python projects that use databases. A long, updated list of such projects is listed on the SQLAlchemy site. Additionally, a pretty good tutorial can be found there, as well. Along with a thin database wrapper, Elixir, it behaves very similarly to the ORM in Rails, ActiveRecord.

External links

- SQLAlchemy [4]
- SQLObject [5]
- PEP 249 [6] - Python Database API Specification v2.0
- Database Topic Guide [7] on python.org

Previous: Web Page Harvesting	Index	Next: Game Programming in Python

References

[1] http://starship.python.net/crew/mhammond/win32/

[2] Hammond, M.;; Robinson, A. (2000). *Python Programming on Win32*. O'Reilly. ISBN 1-56592-621-8.

[3] Lemburg, M.-A. (2007). "Python Database API Specification v2.0" (http://www.python.org/dev/peps/pep-0249/). Python. .

[4] http://www.sqlalchemy.org/

[5] http://www.sqlobject.org/

[6] http://www.python.org/dev/peps/pep-0249/

[7] http://www.python.org/doc/topics/database/

Python Programming/Game Programming in Python

Previous: Database Programming	Index	Next: PyQt4

3D Game Programming

3D Game Engine with a Python binding

- Irrlicht Engine[1] (Python binding website: [2])
- Ogre Engine [3] (Python binding website: [4])

Both are very good free open source C++ 3D game Engine with a Python binding.

- CrystalSpace [5] is a free cross-platform software development kit for realtime 3D graphics, with particular focus on games. Crystal Space is accessible from Python in two ways: (1) as a Crystal Space plugin module in which C++ code can call upon Python code, and in which Python code can call upon Crystal Space; (2) as a pure Python module named 'cspace' which one can 'import' from within Python programs. To use the first option, load the 'cspython' plugin as you would load any other Crystal Space plugin, and interact with it via the SCF 'iScript' interface .The second approach allows you to write Crystal Space applications entirely in Python, without any C++ coding. CS Wiki [6]

3D Game Engines written for Python

Engines designed for Python from scratch.

- Blender [7] is an impressive 3D tool with a fully integrated 3D graphics creation suite allowing modeling, animation, rendering, post-production, realtime interactive 3D and game creation and playback with cross-platform compatibility. The 3D game engine uses an embedded python interpreter to make 3D games.
- Soya [8] is a 3D game engine with an easy to understand design. It's written in the Pyrex programming language and uses Cal3d for animation and ODE for physics. Soya is available under the GNU GPL license.
- PySoy [9] primaly branched from Soya 3D, later rewritten.
- Panda3D [10] is a 3D game engine. It's a library written in C++ with Python bindings. Panda3D is designed in order to support a short learning curve and rapid development. This software is available for free download with source code under the BSD License. The development was started by [Disney]. Now there are many projects made with Panda3D, such as Disney's Pirate's of the Caribbean Online [11], ToonTown [12], Building Virtual World [13], Schell Games [14] and many others. Panda3D supports several features: Procedural Geometry, Animated Texture, Render to texture, Track motion, fog, particle system, and many others.

2D Game Programming

- Pygame is a cross platform Python library which wraps SDL. It provides many features like Sprite groups and sound/image loading and easy changing of an objects position. It also provides the programmer access to key and mouse events.
- Phil's Pygame Utilities (PGU) [15] is a collection of tools and libraries that enhance Pygame. Tools include a tile editor and a level editor (tile, isometric, hexagonal). GUI enhancements include full featured gui, html rendering, document layout, and text rendering. The libraries include a sprite and tile engine (tile, isometric, hexagonal), a state engine, a timer, and a high score system. (Beta with last update March, 2007. APIs to be deprecated and isometric and hexagonal support is currently Alpha and subject to change.) [Update 27/02/08 Author indicates he is not currently actively developing this library and anyone that is willing to develop their own scrolling isometric library offering can use the existing code in PGU to get them started.]
- Pyglet [16] is a cross-platform windowing and multimedia library for Python with no external dependencies or installation requirements. Pyglet provides an object-oriented programming interface for developing games and other visually-rich applications for Windows, Mac OS X and Linux. Pyglet allows programs to open multiple windows on multiple screens, draw in those windows with OpenGL, and play back audio and video in most formats. Unlike similar libraries available, pyglet has no external dependencies (such as SDL) and is written entirely in Python. Pyglet is avaible under a BSD-Style license.
- Rabbyt [17] A fast Sprite library for Python with game development in mind. With Rabbyt Anims, even old graphics cards can produce very fast animations of 2,400 or more sprites handling position, rotation, scaling, and color simultaneously.

See Also

- 10 Lessons Learned [18] - How To Build a Game In A Week From Scratch With No Budget

Previous: Database Programming	Index	Next: PyQt4

References

[1] http://irrlicht.sourceforge.net/
[2] http://pypi.python.org/pypi/pyirrlicht
[3] http://www.ogre3d.org/
[4] http://www.python-ogre.org/
[5] http://www.crystalspace3d.org
[6] http://en.wikipedia.org/wiki/Crystal_Space
[7] http://www.blender.org/
[8] http://www.soya3d.org/
[9] http://www.pysoy.org/
[10] http://www.panda3d.org/
[11] http://disney.go.com/pirates/online/
[12] http://www.toontown.com/
[13] http://www.etc.cmu.edu/bvw
[14] http://www.schellgames.com
[15] http://www.imitationpickles.org/pgu/wiki/index
[16] http://www.pyglet.org/
[17] http://matthewmarshall.org/projects/rabbyt/
[18] http://www.gamedev.net/reference/articles/article2259.asp

Python Programming/PyQt4

Previous: Game Programming in Python	Index	Next: Dbus

WARNING: The examples on this page are a mixture of PyQt3 and PyQt4 - use with caution!

This tutorial aims to provide a hands-on guide to learn the basics of building a small Qt4 application in python.

To follow this tutorial, you should have basic python knowledge, knowledge of Qt4, however, is not necessary. I'm using Linux in these examples and am assuming you already have a working installation of python and pyqt4. To test that, open a python shell by simply typing python in a console to start the interactive interpreter and type

>>> import PyQt4

If this doesn't yield an error message, you should be ready to roll. The examples in this tutorial are kept as easy as possible, showing useful ways to write and structure your program. It is important that you read the source code of the example files, most of the stuff that is done is explained in the code. Use the examples and try to change things, play around with them. This is the best way to get comfortable with it.

Hello, world!

Let's start easy. Popping up a window and displaying something. The following small program will popup a window showing "Hello world!", obviously.

```python
#!/usr/bin/env python


import sys
from PyQt4 import Qt


# We instantiate a QApplication passing the arguments of the script to
it:
a = Qt.QApplication(sys.argv)


# Add a basic widget to this application:
# The first argument is the text we want this QWidget to show, the
second
# one is the parent widget. Since Our "hello" is the only thing we use
(the
# so-called "MainWidget", it does not have a parent.
hello = Qt.QLabel("Hello, World")


# ... and that it should be shown.
hello.show()


# Now we can start it.
a.exec_()
```

About 7 lines of code, and that's about as easy as it can get.

A button

Let's add some interaction! We'll replace the label saying "Hello, World!" with a button and assign an action to it. This assignment is done by connecting a signal, an event which is sent out when the button is pushed to a slot, which is an action, normally a function that is run in the case of that event.

```python
#!/usr/bin/env python

import sys
from PyQt4 import Qt

a = Qt.QApplication(sys.argv)

# Our function to call when the button is clicked
def sayHello():
    print "Hello, World!"

# Instantiate the button
hellobutton = Qt.QPushButton("Say 'Hello world!'",None)

# And connect the action "sayHello" to the event "button has been
clicked"
a.connect(hellobutton, Qt.SIGNAL("clicked()"), sayHello)

# The rest is known already...
#a.setMainWidget(hellobutton)
hellobutton.show()
a.exec_()
```

Urgh, that looks like a crappy approach You can imagine that coding this way is not scalable nor the way you'll want to continue working. So let's make that stuff pythonic, adding structure and actually using object-orientation in it. We create our own application class, derived from a QApplication and put the customization of the application into its methods: One method to build up the widgets and a slot which contains the code that's executed when a signal is received.

```python
#!/usr/bin/env python

import sys
from PyQt4 import Qt

class HelloApplication(Qt.QApplication):

    def __init__(self, args):
        """ In the constructor we're doing everything to get our
application
            started, which is basically constructing a basic
QApplication by
            its __init__ method, then adding our widgets and finally
starting
```

```
            the exec_loop."""
        Qt.QApplication.__init__(self, args)
        self.addWidgets()
        self.exec_()

    def addWidgets(self):
        """ In this method, we're adding widgets and connecting signals
from
            these widgets to methods of our class, the so-called
"slots"
        """
        self.hellobutton = Qt.QPushButton("Say 'Hello world!'",None)
        self.connect(self.hellobutton, Qt.SIGNAL("clicked()"),
self.slotSayHello)
        self.hellobutton.show()

    def slotSayHello(self):
        """ This is an example slot, a method that gets called when a
signal is
            emitted """
        print "Hello, World!"

# Only actually do something if this script is run standalone, so we
can test our
# application, but we're also able to import this program without
actually running
# any code.
if __name__ == "__main__":
    app = HelloApplication(sys.argv)
```

gui coding sucks

... so we want to use Qt3 Designer for creating our GUI. In the picture, you can see a simple GUI, with in green letters the names of the widgets. What we are going to do is We compile the .ui file from Qt designer into a python class We subclass that class and use it as our mainWidget This way, we're able to change the user interface afterwards from Qt designer, without having it messing around in the code we added.

```
pyuic testapp_ui.ui -o testapp_ui.py
```

makes a python file from it which we can work with.

The way our program works can be described like this: We fill in the lineedit Clicking the add button will be connected to a method that reads the text from the lineedit, makes a listviewitem out of it and adds that to our listview. Clicking the deletebutton will delete the currently selected item from the listview. Here's the heavily commented code (only works in PyQt 3:

```
#!/usr/bin/env python

from testapp_ui import TestAppUI
from qt import *
```

```python
import sys

class HelloApplication(QApplication):

    def __init__(self, args):
        """ In the constructor we're doing everything to get our
application
            started, which is basically constructing a basic
QApplication by
            its __init__ method, then adding our widgets and finally
starting
            the exec_loop."""
        QApplication.__init__(self,args)

        # We pass None since it's the top-level widget, we could in
fact leave
        # that one out, but this way it's easier to add more dialogs or
 widgets.
        self.maindialog = TestApp(None)

        self.setMainWidget(self.maindialog)
        self.maindialog.show()
        self.exec_loop()

class TestApp(TestAppUI):

    def __init__(self,parent):
        # Run the parent constructor and connect the slots to methods.
        TestAppUI.__init__(self,parent)
        self._connectSlots()

        # The listview is initially empty, so the deletebutton will
have no effect,
        # we grey it out.
        self.deletebutton.setEnabled(False)

    def _connectSlots(self):
        # Connect our two methods to SIGNALS the GUI emits.
self.connect(self.addbutton,SIGNAL("clicked()"),self._slotAddClicked)

self.connect(self.deletebutton,SIGNAL("clicked()"),self._slotDeleteClicked)

    def _slotAddClicked(self):
        # Read the text from the lineedit,
        text = self.lineedit.text()
        # if the lineedit is not empty,
```

```
        if len(text):
            # insert a new listviewitem ...
            lvi = QListViewItem(self.listview)
            # with the text from the lineedit and ...
            lvi.setText(0,text)
            # clear the lineedit.
            self.lineedit.clear()

            # The deletebutton might be disabled, since we're sure that
there's now
            # at least one item in it, we enable it.
            self.deletebutton.setEnabled(True)

    def _slotDeleteClicked(self):
        # Remove the currently selected item from the listview.
        self.listview.takeItem(self.listview.currentItem())

        # Check if the list is empty - if yes, disable the
deletebutton.
        if self.listview.childCount() == 0:
            self.deletebutton.setEnabled(False)

if __name__ == "__main__":
    app = HelloApplication(sys.argv)
```

useful to know

Creating the GUI in Qt designer does not only make it easier creating the GUI, but it's a great learning tool, too. You can test how a widget looks like, see what's available in Qt and have a look at properties you might want to use.

The C++ API documentation is also a very useful (read: necessary) tool when working with PyQt. The API is translated pretty straightforward, so after having trained a little, you'll find the developers API docs one of the tools you really need. When working from KDE, konqueror's default shortcut is qt:[widgetname], so [alt]+[F2], "qt:qbutton directly takes you to the right API documentation page. Trolltech's doc section has much more documentation which you might want to have a look at.

The first 3 examples in this tutorial have been created using PyQt4, the last one uses syntax that only works with PyQt3.

Note: The previous version of this page (aplicable to pyqt3) is/was available at http://vizzzion.org/?id=pyqt

This document is published under the GNU Free Documentation License.

--84.88.50.161 10:40, 30 November 2006 (UTC) by Saša Tomić, http://galeb.etf.bg.ac.yu/~gospodar

Previous: Game Programming in Python	Index	Next: Dbus

Python Programming/Dbus

Previous: PyQt4	Index	Next: pyFormex

Dbus is a way for processes to communicate with each other. For example, programs like Pidgin [1] instant messenger allow other programs to find out or change the user's status (Available, Away, etc). Another example is the network-manager [2] service that publishes which internet connection is active. Programs that sometimes connect to the internet can then pick the best time to download updates to the system.

Buses

Messages are sent along buses. Services attach themselves to these buses, and allow clients to pass messages to and from them.

There are two main buses, the **system bus** and **session bus**. Services on the system bus affect the whole system, such as providing information about the network or disk drives. Services on the session bus provide access to programs running on the desktop, like Pidgin.

```
import dbus

sys_bus = dbus.SystemBus()
```

Objects and interfaces

Services attached to a bus can be contacted using their **well known name**. While this could be any string, the format is normally that of a reverse domain name: an example for a spreadsheet program called "CalcProgram" from "My Corp Inc." could be "com.mycorp.CalcProgram".

Services publish objects using slash-seperated paths (this is similar to webpages). Someone on dbus can request an object if they know this path.

The object passed back is not a full object: it just refers to the service's copy of the object. It is called a **proxy object**.

```
proxy_for_cell_a2 = sys_bus.get_object('com.mycorp.CalcProgram',
'/spreadsheet1/cells/a2')
```

Before the proxy object can be used, we need to specify what type of object it is. We do this by creating an interface object.

```
cell_a2 = dbus.Interface(proxy_for_cell_a2,
'com.mycorp.CalcProgram.SpreadsheetCell')
```

Whatever methods are set up for this type of object can be called:

```
cell_a2.getContents()
```

Name	Example	Description
service well known name	com.mycorp.CalcProgram	Identifies the application
path of an object	/spreadsheet1/cells/a2	Identifies an object published by a service
interface	com.mycorp.CalcProgram.SpreadsheetCell	Identifies what type of object we expect

Some examples

These examples have been tested with dbus-python 0.83.0. Older library versions may not have the same interface.

Calling an interface's methods / Listing HAL Devices

```
import dbus

bus = dbus.SystemBus()
hal_manager_object = bus.get_object('org.freedesktop.Hal',
'/org/freedesktop/Hal/Manager')
hal_manager_interface = dbus.Interface(hal_manager_object,
'org.freedesktop.Hal.Manager')

# calling method upon interface
print hal_manager_interface.GetAllDevices()

# accessing a method through 'get_dbus_method' through proxy object by
specifying interface
method = hal_manager_object.get_dbus_method('GetAllDevices',
'org.freedesktop.Hal.Manager')
print method()

# calling method upon proxy object by specifying the interface to use
print
hal_manager_object.GetAllDevices(dbus_interface='org.freedesktop.Hal.Manager')
```

Introspecting an object

```
import dbus

bus = dbus.SystemBus()
hal_manager_object = bus.get_object(
    'org.freedesktop.Hal',            # service
    '/org/freedesktop/Hal/Manager'  # published object
)

introspection_interface = dbus.Interface(
    hal_manager_object,
    dbus.INTROSPECTABLE_IFACE,
)
```

```
# Introspectable interfaces define a property 'Introspect' that
# will return an XML string that describes the object's interface
interface = introspection_interface.Introspect()
print interface
```

Avahi

```
import dbus

sys_bus = dbus.SystemBus()

# get an object called / in org.freedesktop.Avahi to talk to
raw_server = sys_bus.get_object('org.freedesktop.Avahi', '/')

# objects support interfaces. get the org.freedesktop.Avahi.Server
# interface to our org.freedesktop.Avahi object.
server = dbus.Interface(raw_server, 'org.freedesktop.Avahi.Server')

# The so-called documentation is at
/usr/share/avahi/introspection/Server.introspect
print server
print server.GetVersionString()
print server.GetHostName()
```

References

- http://www.amk.ca/diary/2007/04/rough_notes_python_and_dbus.html
- http://dbus.freedesktop.org/doc/dbus-tutorial.html
- http://developer.pidgin.im/wiki/DbusHowto
- http://paste.lisp.org/display/45824

Previous: PyQt4	Index	Next: pyFormex

References

[1] http://en.wikipedia.org/wiki/Pidgin_%28software%29
[2] http://en.wikipedia.org/wiki/NetworkManager

Python Programming/pyFormex

Previous: Dbus	Index	Next: Extending with C

pyFormex [1] is a module for Python, which allows the generation, manipulation, and operation of 3D geometric models using mathematical operations. Its uses include automated 3D design and finite-element preprocessing.

Previous: Dbus	Index	Next: Extending with C

References

[1] http://pyformex.berlios.de/

Python Programming/Extending with C

Previous: pyFormex	Index	Next: Extending with C++

This gives a minimal Example on how to Extend Python with C. Linux is used for building (feel free to extend it for other Platforms). If you have any problems, please report them (e.g. on the dicussion page), I will check back in a while and try to sort them out.

Using the Python/C API

*   http://docs.python.org/ext/ext.html
*   http://docs.python.org/api/api.html

A minimal example

The minimal example we will create now is very similar in behaviour to the following python snippet:

```python
def say_hello(name):
    "Greet somebody."
    print "Hello %s!" % name
```

The C source code (hellomodule.c)

```c
#include <Python.h>

static PyObject* say_hello(PyObject* self, PyObject* args)
{
    const char* name;

    if (!PyArg_ParseTuple(args, "s", &name))
        return NULL;

    printf("Hello %s!\n", name);
```

```
    Py_RETURN_NONE;
}


static PyMethodDef HelloMethods[] =
{
    {"say_hello", say_hello, METH_VARARGS, "Greet somebody."},
    {NULL, NULL, 0, NULL}
};


PyMODINIT_FUNC

inithello(void)
{
    (void) Py_InitModule("hello", HelloMethods);
}
```

Building the extension module with GCC for Linux

To build our extension module we create the file setup.py like:

```
from distutils.core import setup, Extension

module1 = Extension('hello', sources = ['hellomodule.c'])

setup (name = 'PackageName',
       version = '1.0',
       description = 'This is a demo package',
       ext_modules = [module1])
```

Now we can build our module with

```
python setup.py build
```

The module hello.so will end up in build/lib.linux-i686-*x*.*y*.

Building the extension module with GCC for Microsoft Windows

Microsoft Windows users can use MinGW to compile this from cmd.exe using a similar method to Linux user, as shown above. Assuming gcc is in the PATH environment variable, type:

```
python setup.py build -c mingw32
```

The module hello.pyd will end up in build\lib.win32-*x*.*y*, which is a Python Dynamic Module (similar to a DLL).

An alternate way of building the module in Windows is to build a DLL. (This method does not need an extension module file). From cmd.exe, type:

```
gcc -c  hellomodule.c -I/PythonXY/include
gcc -shared hellomodule.o -L/PythonXY/libs -lpythonXY -o hello.dll
```

where *XY* represents the version of Python, such as "24" for version 2.4.

Building the extension module using Microsoft Visual C++

With VC8 distutils is broken. We will use cl.exe from a command prompt instead:

```
cl /LD hellomodule.c /Ic:\Python24\include c:\Python24\libs\python24.lib /link/out:hello.dll
```

Using the extension module

Change to the subdirectory where the file `hello.so` resides. In an interactive python session you can use the module as follows.

```
>>> import hello
>>> hello.say_hello("World")
Hello World!
```

A module for calculating fibonacci numbers

The C source code (fibmodule.c)

```c
#include <Python.h>

int _fib(int n)
{
    if (n < 2)
        return n;
    else
        return _fib(n-1) + _fib(n-2);
}

static PyObject* fib(PyObject* self, PyObject* args)
{
    const char *command;
    int n;

    if (!PyArg_ParseTuple(args, "i", &n))
        return NULL;

    return Py_BuildValue("i", _fib(n));
}

static PyMethodDef FibMethods[] = {
    {"fib", fib, METH_VARARGS, "Calculate the Fibonacci numbers."},
    {NULL, NULL, 0, NULL}
};

PyMODINIT_FUNC
initfib(void)
{
    (void) Py_InitModule("fib", FibMethods);
}
```

The build script (setup.py)

```
from distutils.core import setup, Extension

module1 = Extension('fib', sources = ['fibmodule.c'])

setup (name = 'PackageName',
       version = '1.0',
       description = 'This is a demo package',
       ext_modules = [module1])
```

How to use it?

```
>>> import fib
>>> fib.fib(10)
55
```

Using SWIG

Creating the previous example using SWIG is much more straight forward. To follow this path you need to get SWIG [1] up and running first. After that create two files.

```
/*hellomodule.c*/

#include <stdio.h>

void say_hello(const char* name) {
    printf("Hello %s!\n", name);
}
```

```
/*hello.i*/

%module hello
extern void say_hello(const char* name);
```

Now comes the more difficult part, gluing it all together.

First we need to let SWIG do its work.

```
swig -python hello.i
```

This gives us the files `hello.py` and `hello_wrap.c`.

The next step is compiling (substitute /usr/include/python2.4/ with the correct path for your setup!).

```
gcc -fpic -c hellomodule.c hello_wrap.c -I/usr/include/python2.4/
```

Now linking and we are done!

```
gcc -shared hellomodule.o hello_wrap.o -o _hello.so
```

The module is used in the following way.

```
>>> import hello
>>> hello.say_hello("World")
Hello World!
```

Previous: pyFormex	Index	Next: Extending with C++

References

[1] http://www.swig.org/

Python Programming/Extending with C++

Previous: Extending with C	Index	Next: Extending with Pyrex

Boost.Python [1] is the de facto standard for writing C++ extension modules. Boost.Python comes bundled with the Boost C++ Libraries [2].

The C++ source code (hellomodule.cpp)

```cpp
#include <iostream>

using namespace std;

void say_hello(const char* name) {
    cout << "Hello " <<  name << "!\n";
}

#include <boost/python/module.hpp>
#include <boost/python/def.hpp>
using namespace boost::python;

BOOST_PYTHON_MODULE(hello)
{
    def("say_hello", say_hello);
}
```

setup.py

```python
#!/usr/bin/env python

from distutils.core import setup
from distutils.extension import Extension

setup(name="blah",
    ext_modules=[
        Extension("hello", ["hellomodule.cpp"],
        libraries = ["boost_python"])
    ])
```

Now we can build our module with

```
python setup.py build
```

The module `hello.so` will end up in e.g `build/lib.linux-i686-2.4`.

Using the extension module

Change to the subdirectory where the file `hello.so` resides. In an interactive python session you can use the module as follows.

```
>>> import hello
>>> hello.say_hello("World")
Hello World!
```

Previous: Extending with C	Index	Next: Extending with Pyrex

References

[1] http://www.boost.org/libs/python/doc/
[2] http://www.boost.org/

Python Programming/Extending with Pyrex

Previous: Extending with C++	Index	Next: Extending with ctypes

Previous: Extending with C++	Index	Next: Extending with ctypes

Python Programming/Extending with ctypes

| Previous: Extending with Pyrex | Index |

ctypes[1] is a foreign function interface module for Python (included with Python 2.5 and above), which allows you to load in dynamic libraries and call C functions. This is not technically extending Python, but it serves one of the primary reasons for extending Python: to interface with external C code.

Basics

A library is loaded using the ctypes.CDLL function. After you load the library, the functions inside the library are already usable as regular Python calls. For example, if we wanted to forego the standard Python print statement and use the standard C library function, printf, you would use this:

```
from ctypes import *
libName = 'libc.so' # If you're on a UNIX-based system
libName = 'msvcrt.dll' # If you're on Windows
libc = CDLL(libName)
libc.printf("Hello, World!\n")
```

Of course, you must use the libName line that matches your operating system, and delete the other. If all goes well, you should see the infamous Hello World string at your console.

Getting Return Values

ctypes assumes, by default, that any given function's return type is a signed integer of native size. Sometimes you don't want the function to return anything, and other times, you want the function to return other types. Every ctypes function has an attribute called restype. When you assign a ctypes class to restype, it automatically casts the function's return value to that type.

Common Types

ctypes name	C type	Python type	Notes
None	void	None	the None object
c_bool	C99 _Bool	bool	
c_byte	signed char	int	
c_char	signed char	str	length of one
c_char_p	char *	str	
c_double	double	float	
c_float	float	float	
c_int	signed int	int	
c_long	signed long	long	
c_longlong	signed long long	long	
c_short	signed short	long	
c_ubyte	unsigned char	int	
c_uint	unsigned int	int	

c_ulong	unsigned long	long	
c_ulonglong	unsigned long long	long	
c_ushort	unsigned short	int	
c_void_p	void *	int	
c_wchar	wchar_t	unicode	length of one
c_wchar_p	wchar_t *	unicode	

Previous: Extending with Pyrex	Index

References

[1] http://python.net/crew/theller/ctypes/

Article Sources and Contributors

Python Programming/Overview *Source*: http://en.wikibooks.org/w/index.php?oldid=1738642 *Contributors*: Artevelde, BobGibson, CWii, Cspurrier, Darklama, DavidRoss, Flarelocke, IO, Jguk, Leopold augustsson, Remi0o, Remote, Sigma 7, Withinfocus, Yath, 13 anonymous edits

Python Programming/Getting Python *Source*: http://en.wikibooks.org/w/index.php?oldid=1786943 *Contributors*: Artevelde, CWii, Darklama, Dragonecc, Greyweather, Jguk, Leopold augustsson, Mr.Z-man, Mshonle, Panic2k4, Sigma 7, Tecky2, The djinn, Thunderbolt16, Withinfocus, Yath, 40 anonymous edits

Python Programming/Setting it up *Source*: http://en.wikibooks.org/w/index.php?oldid=1753061 *Contributors*: BoomShaka, Leopold augustsson, Mr.Z-man, MyOwnLittlWorld, Rabidgoldfish, The djinn, 9 anonymous edits

Python Programming/Interactive mode *Source*: http://en.wikibooks.org/w/index.php?oldid=1738665 *Contributors*: Artevelde, BobGibson, Darklama, IO, Jguk, Leopold augustsson, Mr.Z-man, Sigma 7, The djinn, Withinfocus, Yath, 4 anonymous edits

Python Programming/Self Help *Source*: http://en.wikibooks.org/w/index.php?oldid=1721616 *Contributors*: Mr.Z-man, Sigma 7, The Kid, 3 anonymous edits

Python Programming/Creating Python programs *Source*: http://en.wikibooks.org/w/index.php?oldid=1647561 *Contributors*: Adeelq, Artevelde, BobGibson, CWii, Chesemonkyloma, Darklama, DavidRoss, Deep shobhit, Dragonecc, JackPotte, Jguk, Legoktm, MMJ, ManuelGR, Mattzazami, Mr.Z-man, Nikai, QuiteUnusual, Richard001, Sigma 7, Singingwolfboy, Thunderbolt16, Wenhaosparty, Withinfocus, Yath, 15 anonymous edits

Python Programming/Basic Math *Source*: http://en.wikibooks.org/w/index.php?oldid=1893189 *Contributors*: AdriMartin, Beland, CWii, Cat1205123, Fishpi, Jesdisciple, Jomegat, Monobi, Rancid, Sigma 7, Singingwolfboy, Wesley Gray, 10 anonymous edits

Python Programming/Decision Control *Source*: http://en.wikibooks.org/w/index.php?oldid=1796615 *Contributors*: Beland, Capi, Darklama, DavidRoss, ElieDeBrauwer, GeorgePatterson, Jesdisciple, Jguk, Mediocretes, Niflhiem, Sigma 7, Webaware, 17 anonymous edits

Python Programming/Conditional Statements *Source*: http://en.wikibooks.org/w/index.php?oldid=1875314 *Contributors*: CWii, DavidRoss, Dobau, Dragonecc, ElieDeBrauwer, Gabrielmagno, Gzorg, Mithrill2002, Monobi, Moralist, Mr.Z-man, NithinBekal, Piperrob, Sigma 7, Svenstaro, Webaware, 35 anonymous edits

Python Programming/Loops *Source*: http://en.wikibooks.org/w/index.php?oldid=1796630 *Contributors*: Amrik, Bluecanary, CWii, Chenhsi, DavidRoss, ElieDeBrauwer, Gvdraconatur, Hrandiac, Hypergeek14, Jesdisciple, Jguk, Mithrill2002, Monobi, Mr.Z-man, Richard001, Sigma 7, Webaware, 11 anonymous edits

Python Programming/Sequences *Source*: http://en.wikibooks.org/w/index.php?oldid=1796653 *Contributors*: Beland, CWii, ElieDeBrauwer, Fef, Jesdisciple, Jonnymbarnes, Mr.Z-man, Sigma 7, Silroquen, Singingwolfboy, The Kid, 9 anonymous edits

Python Programming/Source Documentation and Comments *Source*: http://en.wikibooks.org/w/index.php?oldid=1891782 *Contributors*: CWii, Hypergeek14, Jesdisciple, Mr.Z-man, Quartz25, Sigma 7, Webaware, 2 anonymous edits

Python Programming/Modules and how to use them *Source*: http://en.wikibooks.org/w/index.php?oldid=1430705 *Contributors*: CWii, DavidRoss, Dlrohrer2003, Hypergeek14, Monobi, Mr.Z-man, Pjerrot, Sigma 7, 5 anonymous edits

Python Programming/Files *Source*: http://en.wikibooks.org/w/index.php?oldid=1799118 *Contributors*: CWii, Darklama, Dbolton, ElieDeBrauwer, Jguk, LDiracDelta, Monobi, Mr.Z-man, Webaware, Withinfocus, 11 anonymous edits

Python Programming/Text *Source*: http://en.wikibooks.org/w/index.php?oldid=1893212 *Contributors*: I-20, Mr.Z-man, 1 anonymous edits

Python Programming/Errors *Source*: http://en.wikibooks.org/w/index.php?oldid=1758135 *Contributors*: Albmont, Beland, Gvdraconatur, Icewedge, Mr.Z-man, 2 anonymous edits

Python Programming/Namespace *Source*: http://en.wikibooks.org/w/index.php?oldid=1410921 *Contributors*: Hypergeek14, Mr.Z-man, 1 anonymous edits

Python Programming/Object-oriented programming *Source*: http://en.wikibooks.org/w/index.php?oldid=1811180 *Contributors*: Alexforcefive, CWii, Capi, Dragonecc, ElieDeBrauwer, Hypergeek14, Keplerspeed, Marjoe, Mr.Z-man, Piperrob, Sigma 7, 9 anonymous edits

Python Programming/User Interaction *Source*: http://en.wikibooks.org/w/index.php?oldid=1886374 *Contributors*: Dragonecc, Horaceabenga, Hypergeek14, Mr.Z-man, Pereirai, Piperrob, Sigma 7, 10 anonymous edits

Python Programming/Databases *Source*: http://en.wikibooks.org/w/index.php?oldid=1808711 *Contributors*: Hannes Röst, Hypergeek14, Mr.Z-man, 3 anonymous edits

Python Programming/Internet *Source*: http://en.wikibooks.org/w/index.php?oldid=1428307 *Contributors*: Kuzux, Monobi, Mr.Z-man, Webaware, 4 anonymous edits

Python Programming/Networks *Source*: http://en.wikibooks.org/w/index.php?oldid=1410932 *Contributors*: Hypergeek14, Mr.Z-man, 3 anonymous edits

Python Programming/Tips and Tricks *Source*: http://en.wikibooks.org/w/index.php?oldid=1741352 *Contributors*: Chelseafan528, Darklama, Hakusa, Hawk-McKain, Hypergeek14, Jguk, Member, Microdot, Mr.Z-man, Pazabo, Ponstic, Quartz25, The Kid, The djinn, Webaware, 8 anonymous edits

Python Programming/Basic syntax *Source*: http://en.wikibooks.org/w/index.php?oldid=1867990 *Contributors*: Artevelde, BobGibson, Darklama, Flarelocke, Hypergeek14, Jguk, Mr.Z-man, Nikai, Rdnk, Richard001, The Kid, Thunderbolt16, Webaware, Withinfocus, 9 anonymous edits

Python Programming/Data types *Source*: http://en.wikibooks.org/w/index.php?oldid=1410936 *Contributors*: Adriatikus, Artevelde, Darklama, Flarelocke, Jguk, Mr.Z-man, Thunderbolt16, Webaware, Withinfocus, Yath, 9 anonymous edits

Python Programming/Numbers *Source*: http://en.wikibooks.org/w/index.php?oldid=1511185 *Contributors*: Artevelde, Brian McErlean, Darklama, Irvin.sha, Jguk, Thunderbolt16, Webaware, Withinfocus, 7 anonymous edits

Python Programming/Strings *Source*: http://en.wikibooks.org/w/index.php?oldid=1810270 *Contributors*: Artevelde, Chuckhoffmann, Daemonax, Darklama, Flarelocke, IO, Irvin.sha, Jguk, Mithrill2002, Remote, Webaware, Withinfocus, 88 anonymous edits

Python Programming/Lists *Source*: http://en.wikibooks.org/w/index.php?oldid=1872500 *Contributors*: Artevelde, Hannes Röst, Jguk, LDiracDelta, Offpath, Rdnk, Remote, Richard001, Robm351, Thunderbolt16, Webaware, Withinfocus, 27 anonymous edits

Python Programming/Tuples *Source*: http://en.wikibooks.org/w/index.php?oldid=1639579 *Contributors*: Adamnelson, Alexdong, Artevelde, Jguk, LDiracDelta, Mr.Z-man, Remote, Thunderbolt16, Webaware, Withinfocus, 8 anonymous edits

Python Programming/Dictionaries *Source*: http://en.wikibooks.org/w/index.php?oldid=1667221 *Contributors*: Artevelde, Fry-kun, Jguk, Remote, Thunderbolt16, Webaware, Withinfocus, 13 anonymous edits

Python Programming/Sets *Source*: http://en.wikibooks.org/w/index.php?oldid=1402487 *Contributors*: ArrowStomper, Artevelde, FerranJorba, Jguk, Mr.Z-man, Webaware, Withinfocus, 2 anonymous edits

Python Programming/Operators *Source*: http://en.wikibooks.org/w/index.php?oldid=1841460 *Contributors*: Artevelde, Beland, Benrolfe, Dbolton, Flarelocke, Hannes Röst, Irvin.sha, Jguk, Remote, Thunderbolt16, Webaware, Withinfocus, 10 anonymous edits

Python Programming/Flow control *Source*: http://en.wikibooks.org/w/index.php?oldid=1679989 *Contributors*: Alexander256, Artevelde, Flarelocke, Gasto5, Hannes Röst, Jguk, MarceloAraujo, Remote, Thunderbolt16, Webaware, Withinfocus, 30 anonymous edits

Python Programming/Functions *Source*: http://en.wikibooks.org/w/index.php?oldid=1759216 *Contributors*: Albmont, Artevelde, Cburnett, Darklama, Flarelocke, JackPotte, Jerf, Jguk, Jonathan Webley, MarceloAraujo, Mr.Z-man, The Kid, Webaware, Withinfocus, 4 anonymous edits

Python Programming/Decorators *Source*: http://en.wikibooks.org/w/index.php?oldid=1752675 *Contributors*: Codesmith111, Mr.Z-man, The Kid, 2 anonymous edits

Python Programming/Scoping *Source*: http://en.wikibooks.org/w/index.php?oldid=1410942 *Contributors*: Artevelde, Flarelocke, Jguk, Mr.Z-man, Qwertyus, The Kid, Webaware, Withinfocus, 3 anonymous edits

Python Programming/Exceptions *Source*: http://en.wikibooks.org/w/index.php?oldid=1618744 *Contributors*: Artevelde, Behnam, Betalpha, Flarelocke, Jguk, Microdot, Nikai, The djinn, Thunderbolt16, Tobych, Webaware, Withinfocus, 18 anonymous edits

Python Programming/Input and output *Source*: http://en.wikibooks.org/w/index.php?oldid=1804360 *Contributors*: Artevelde, Az1568, Betalpha, DavidCary, Flarelocke, Jguk, LDiracDelta, Pavlix, Qwertyus, Tedzzz1, Webaware, Withinfocus, 20 anonymous edits

Python Programming/Modules *Source*: http://en.wikibooks.org/w/index.php?oldid=1661792 *Contributors*: Artevelde, Eric Silva, Flarelocke, Hannes Röst, Jguk, MarceloAraujo, Webaware, Withinfocus, 6 anonymous edits

Python Programming/Classes *Source*: http://en.wikibooks.org/w/index.php?oldid=1873695 *Contributors*: Adrignola, Albmont, Apeigne, Artevelde, Darklama, Flarelocke, Hannes Röst, Jerf, Jguk, Microdot, Perey, Webaware, Withinfocus, 39 anonymous edits

Python Programming/MetaClasses *Source*: http://en.wikibooks.org/w/index.php?oldid=1410945 *Contributors*: Artevelde, Convex, Darklama, Hypergeek14, Jguk, Mr.Z-man, Quartz25, Webaware, Withinfocus, 7 anonymous edits

Python Programming/Standard Library *Source*: http://en.wikibooks.org/w/index.php?oldid=1758086 *Contributors*: Albmont, Darklama, Jguk, Mr.Z-man, 2 anonymous edits

Python Programming/Regular Expression *Source*: http://en.wikibooks.org/w/index.php?oldid=1484385 *Contributors*: Beland, Darklama, Jguk, Mr.Z-man, Mwtoews, Withinfocus, 5 anonymous edits

Python Programming/XML Tools *Source*: http://en.wikibooks.org/w/index.php?oldid=1420988 *Contributors*: CWii, Hypergeek14, Monobi, Mr.Z-man, The djinn, Webaware, Wilsondavidc

Python Programming/Email *Source*: http://en.wikibooks.org/w/index.php?oldid=1420990 *Contributors*: Mr.Z-man

Python Programming/Threading *Source*: http://en.wikibooks.org/w/index.php?oldid=1854836 *Contributors*: Hannes Röst, Howipepper, Hypergeek14, Jguk, Mr.Z-man, Quartz25, Webaware, Withinfocus, 11 anonymous edits

Python Programming/Sockets *Source*: http://en.wikibooks.org/w/index.php?oldid=1810615 *Contributors*: Ahornedal, CWii, Darklama, Hagindaz, Howipepper, Hypergeek14, Jguk, Mr.Z-man, Webaware, WikiNazi, Wilbur.harvey, Withinfocus, 2 anonymous edits

Python Programming/GUI Programming *Source*: http://en.wikibooks.org/w/index.php?oldid=1681118 *Contributors*: Albmont, Auk, Baijum81, CWii, Darklama, Edleafe, Guanaco, Gutworth, Jguk, Mr.Z-man, N313t3, NithinBekal, Pingveno, Suchenwi, The djinn, Withinfocus, 28 anonymous edits

Python Programming/WSGI web programming *Source*: http://en.wikibooks.org/w/index.php?oldid=1559332 *Contributors*: CaffeinatedPonderer, Dragonecc, Hypergeek14, Mr.Z-man

Python Programming/Web Page Harvesting *Source*: http://en.wikibooks.org/w/index.php?oldid=1410956 *Contributors*: Hypergeek14, Mr.Z-man

Python Programming/Database Programming *Source*: http://en.wikibooks.org/w/index.php?oldid=1800239 *Contributors*: Darklama, Hypergeek14, Jguk, Mr.Z-man, Mwtoews, Sol, The djinn, Webaware, Withinfocus, 3 anonymous edits

Python Programming/Game Programming in Python *Source*: http://en.wikibooks.org/w/index.php?oldid=1853171 *Contributors*: CWii, Darklama, Derbeth, Driscoll, Hypergeek14, Jguk, Kernigh, Maxim kolosov, Mr.Z-man, N313t3, Pdilley, Webaware, Withinfocus, 40 anonymous edits

Python Programming/PyQt4 *Source*: http://en.wikibooks.org/w/index.php?oldid=1691989 *Contributors*: Danh, Herbythyme, Mr.Z-man, Sasa.tomic, 15 anonymous edits

Python Programming/Dbus *Source*: http://en.wikibooks.org/w/index.php?oldid=1800134 *Contributors*: Dangets, H2g2bob, Mr.Z-man, 5 anonymous edits

Python Programming/pyFormex *Source*: http://en.wikibooks.org/w/index.php?oldid=1410963 *Contributors*: CaffeinatedPonderer, Mr.Z-man

Python Programming/Extending with C *Source*: http://en.wikibooks.org/w/index.php?oldid=1629564 *Contributors*: Adrignola, CWii, Darklama, Hagindaz, Jguk, Mr.Z-man, Mwtoews, Myururdurmaz, Webaware, Withinfocus, 30 anonymous edits

Python Programming/Extending with C++ *Source*: http://en.wikibooks.org/w/index.php?oldid=1410967 *Contributors*: CWii, Darklama, Jguk, Mr.Z-man, Panic2k4, Webaware, Withinfocus, 2 anonymous edits

Python Programming/Extending with Pyrex *Source*: http://en.wikibooks.org/w/index.php?oldid=1410968 *Contributors*: CWii, Mr.Z-man

Python Programming/Extending with ctypes *Source*: http://en.wikibooks.org/w/index.php?oldid=1410971 *Contributors*: CaffeinatedPonderer, Hypergeek14, Mr.Z-man, Quartz25, Webaware

Image Sources, Licenses and Contributors

Image:Crystal_Clear_action_bookmark.png *Source*: http://en.wikibooks.org/w/index.php?title=File:Crystal_Clear_action_bookmark.png *License*: unknown *Contributors*: Abu badali, Actam, Airon90, Anime Addict AA, CyberSkull, EDUCA33E, It Is Me Here, Juiced lemon, Rocket000, Tiptoety, 2 anonymous edits

Image:Information icon.svg *Source*: http://en.wikibooks.org/w/index.php?title=File:Information_icon.svg *License*: unknown *Contributors*: El T

License

Printed in Great Britain
by Amazon.co.uk, Ltd.,
Marston Gate.